The Burning Bush:
Speeches by Elias Simojoki

THE BURNING BUSH

—Palava Pensas—

SPEECHES BY

ELIAS SIMOJOKI

Translated by Jarno Alander

ANTELOPE HILL PUBLISHING

Second printing 2022.

Compiled by Vilho Helanen
Foreword and Introduction by Vilho Helanen
Originally published by Werner Söderström Osakeyhtiö, Helsinki 1942.
Original English translation 2021 by Jarno Alander, with thanks to
Teemu Lahtinen for his historical expertise

Cover art by Swifty
Edited and formatted by Margaret Bauer

Antelope Hill Publishing
antelopehillpublishing.com

Paperback ISBN-13: 978-1-956887-29-7
EPUB ISBN-13: 978-1-953730-59-6

Contents

Foreword

By Vilho Helanen

Elias Simojoki was a nationalist fighter, and as such his lot in life was to be controversial. But only now that his life's work is concluded, can we fully appreciate it.

Simojoki's main influence was as a leader of youth. Undeniably he was one of the most significant moral leaders that Finland's youth have ever had. His influence on the educated youth of our country has been decisive in the last two decades. In previous years, that youth, and especially its most active members, have encountered significant criticism. At times their potential has been dismissed as wasted, at others they have been derided as being misguided. To many of previous generations, the new youth have seemed alien in their thoughts, ideals, and attitudes toward life.

However, ever since the fall of 1939, this estimation has changed. As officers fighting on the front lines during the Winter War, the men of our present generation achieved the respect of our nation. Our present struggle[1] has only fortified that respect. No one would make the mistake of calling them a wasted generation any longer. Their achievements show that the influences and the leadership that made them who they are were overwhelmingly positive and correct. But where do these ideals, thoughts, and attitudes, that have now proven their worth in the great trial by fire of our nation, come from? And what exactly do they include in the final analysis?

These questions without a doubt will direct our attention to

---

[1] The "present struggle" referred to is the Continuation War, between Finland and the Soviet Union. The conflict took place between 1941 and 1944.

Elias Simojoki, who was their fiercest advocate, and whose life's work received its final seal, when he joined the heroic dead on the ice of Lake Ladoga[2], on January 25, 1940. The strength of our entire nation is now focused on making Greater Finland[3] a reality. We have entered the decisive battle for life or death, which Simojoki tirelessly insisted was inevitable. For many, it seems a great defeat for our nation that he is no longer among our ranks. But he lives on in his writings and speeches. His life's work, as an appeal to the Finnish people, has never been more timely than now. His speeches also contain many observations regarding our national rise and awakening that will remain of value and interest far into the future.

The present collection by no means contains all of Simojoki's speeches. Most of his work as a public speaker was carried out as a priest — which, after all, was his principal occupation. His fierce sermons and speeches at conventicles will not soon be forgotten by those who had the privilege of hearing them in life. This tome contains only a couple of those, which some readers may consider a fault. However, the main purpose of this compilation is to bring together his speeches that deal with nationalism and patriotism. Besides, it was only very rarely that Simojoki wrote his religious sermons down, beyond brief notes and outlines.

No actual writings authored by Simojoki have been included. The one exception to this is the very first piece, "Do You Remember," in which he describes the origins of his nationalist evangelical work in a heartfelt, almost shocking manner.

The time has not yet come for a full biography of Elias Simojoki. However, I have seen it fit to explain his life and work briefly, in an anecdotal manner. I hope the following pages can in some way illuminate the background of his speeches. I have received valuable aid and support in my work from the widow of

---

[2] Ladoga (Finnish Laatokka) lake in Karelia. It is the largest lake in Europe.
[3] Greater Finland (*Suur-Suomi*) is an idea that Finland's geographical area should be expanded (by aggressive military means if necessary) to include all areas historically inhabited by the Finno-Baltic tribes. It had significant support between the Finnish independence (1917) and World War II, but largely fell out of favor after WWII.

my late friend, Mrs. Liisa Simojoki, from his sister Mrs. Rakel Terä, and from his brother, Vicar Arvi Simojoki, and I am deeply grateful to them.

Introduction

By Vilho Helanen

Elias Simojoki was born into the famous Simelius family of clergymen, in the chaplain's parsonage of Rautio, on January 28, 1899. He was an exceptionally beautiful and active child, winning the hearts of all around the parsonage. All of his well-known personality traits, which later in life would win people's hearts over to him, were already apparent at the time. He was gregarious by nature and crystal clear in his soul. From childhood on he had an especially close relationship with God. It was not enough for him to confess his misdeeds to his parents in the evening before bed and ask for their forgiveness. He also took stock of his daily activities with the heavenly Father in his evening prayers. He was a regular attendee in church already as a small boy and often took part in conventicles. During his school years, the religious influences he received at home solidified into a decision that led him onto the path of a deep religious awakening.

He was warm-hearted and helpful already as a small child. He was especially fond of animals. The stable and barn at the parsonage were an entire world for him, one he loved to spend time in. This tenderness followed him through his entire life, and after all, it was the cries of pain of a wounded horse that finally led him to death on the ice of Lake Ladoga.

Simojoki attended the Finnish lyceum of the town of Oulu, where his wits and courage brought him the respect of his peers. He was often the winner in the boys' rough games and competitions. He became the leader of his group of comrades and was always there to give them advice or counsel. His activities were always based on his early ideological awakening. He was a leading force in the sobriety society of his school's student association. He was the spokesman for both of these and also wrote for the student association magazine. At home he had already published his own little magazine, publishing in it writings which evidenced his sense of humor, which he became well known for later in life. At the lyceum, his lively writing style drew the attention of teachers, and his literary interests occupied a significant amount of his time. During this period, he was still very much a man of the written (as opposed to the spoken) word. It was not until the seventh grade that he gave a presentation on Tagore and his poetry at the annual celebration of the student association. The literary endeavors of his school years were crowned with his matriculation examination essay, "Blessed be the Peacemakers," which already bore all the hallmarks of his literary style. The principal message of his essay was that it is possible to create peace with arms. Surprisingly, given how far removed from the current ideas of the time, his essay was given the highest grade, laudatur.[4]

His profound interest in history, especially Finnish military history, was also already apparent in his childhood. He read all the literature on this topic that was available to him, and his writings as a schoolboy often dealt with it. As his family was living in Rantsila he often skied or rode around the countryside houses, his mind glowing with memories of the battles the Finnish army fought there in 1808-09. He was always excited when his father brought him along to Siikajoki to see the old battlefield, and he had the opportunity to examine the ancient, rusty weapons that still remained in the houses of the area. An interest in old weapons followed him throughout his entire life, and over the years he accumulated quite a collection of them.

Elias Simojoki was in the seventh grade when the Freedom

---

[4] The matriculation examination grades are, from highest to lowest, *laudatur, eximia cum laude approbatur, magna cum laude approbatur, cum laude approbatur, lubenter approbatur, approbatur* and *improbatur* (failed exam)

War[5] broke out. It was natural that he should be among the first to join the liberation army. As a member of the First Oulu Company,[6] he took part in all of its battles. His many speeches that refer to his experiences in the company ranks clearly show how these months left a profound mark on his sensitive mind.

He finished his studies in 1919. He could barely wait till the end of the exams — in the end, he left them unfinished for the time being — because his mind already yearned for the warpath. For him, this time it was about the freedom cause of our tribal kin from beyond the border. The Eastern Karelians had already risen up in 1918 to push back the tidal wave of Slavic communism, and in late winter 1919, the battles intensified. Officially Finland had little sympathy for the struggle, but many Finnish volunteers rushed to assist in the rise of Olonets[7]. Without hesitation, Simojoki joined the volunteers from Oulu. The stages of this struggle are well-known by now, a quick advance toward the south toward the river Svir[8] and then eastward toward Petrozavodsk was interrupted when the enemy roused a great force for a counter-attack. The victorious moments shared with the civilians of Olonets, exciting patrol trips that taxed his physical and mental strength to their very limits, and finally, the collapse of their shared hopes together, was an experience he never managed to overcome.

Simojoki joined the theological faculty of the University of Helsinki in fall 1919. However, his studies were interrupted again. The flame of the freedom struggle was lit again in Eastern Karelia in 1921. Once again, Simojoki did not hesitate, left his studies and joined the Finnish volunteers. He was a part of a ranger operation, who crossed the border and were to penetrate deep beyond enemy lines, and to demolish a railroad bridge crossing Svir. Once

---

[5] The war Simojoki refers to as the "Freedom War" is the war today referred to as the Finnish Civil War of 1918.

[6] At its formation this company consisted of 207 men. Later in the war it became the third company of the so-called Northern Ostrobothnian Regiment.

[7] In Finnish known as "Aunus," this name refers both to a town in Karelia and the region of which it is the administrative center.

[8] A river that connects the Ladoga and Onega lakes.

again, the Karelian-Finnish troops had initial success, especially in the White Sea area, with town after town being liberated. However, the Bolsheviks sent a well-armed force that outnumbered the poorly-armed volunteers by ten. No additional assistance was given from Finland, and thus in January and February 1922, the fate of the final armed rebellion in Eastern Karelia was sealed. Therefore, the ranger party that Simojoki belonged to had to return, their mission unaccomplished.

A certain comrade has recorded Simojoki's thought at the time of defeat:

> *A taxing retreat from Olonets across the border has been carried out. Heavy casualties. Our vision grows dim. Has the part of freedom for Karelia been blocked? Is Greater Finland dead? This is what Elias Simojoki asks himself again and again, in great anxiety. Never. Greater Finland will not die. Karelia must be allowed to live and to triumph. But how? Simojoki found the answer in the hearts of Finland's youth. The dream becomes clear, a dream of a fighting, militant youth, who once will walk the path of sacrifice victoriously. The road opens toward the dawn, the dawn of Greater Finland. It is a twisting path. A voice calls, this is the only salvation. A boy leaves, and a man comes forward instead, and sets on the path of struggle and sacrifice: Elias Simojoki.*

He had left for battle as a youth, almost a boy, but returned a man, who resolved to continue fighting against all odds. It was on the battlefields of Olonets, that his great idea of Greater Finland was born, and the youth were to make it a reality. The tool for the task that he created seemed very modest at first: it was with two comrades who had returned from Karelia along with him that he created the Akateeminen Karjala-Seura (Academic Karelia Society, AKS).

15 years later he described the founding of this association of militant activists:

As has been pointed out before, those Finnish students who founded the AKS, returned from the freedom fight of Karelia with shell-shocked minds. They could not, even in the midst of all the frivolity in our capital, forget the suffering of our tribe that they were forced to witness in Karelia. The battle they had taken part in was a holy war for the life or death of our people. The present writer can remember to this day, how we read Bible verses from Daily Watchwords and muttered silent prayers to Him, who held the keys to our life or death.

At the gates of death, in the silence of the wilderness, in the destroyed villages of Karelia — this is where the founding words of the AKS were spoken. Faced with the limitless hardship that closed the way to Karelian freedom, a man had to recognize his own weakness and understand that the grace of God is the only hope and aid for an individual and a nation.

At first, the AKS agenda did not mention the true objectives of its young founders. They described the purpose of the association as offering material and spiritual aid for the refugees who had arrived to our country from Eastern Karelia. One would think that even *that* would be enough for a tiny organization of university students. But Elias Simojoki set his aim much higher. He never considered the possibility that the AKS might be just another student association, among many others. He created it as a brotherhood, whose members would continue fighting toward the great objective throughout their lives.

This is made clear in the flag oath of the AKS, largely penned by Simojoki himself.

Under our flag, and to our flag I swear, by all that is dear and valuable to me, to sacrifice my life and labor to my Fatherland, to its national awakening, for Karelia and Ingria, for Greater Finland. For as much as I believe in one almighty God, I believe in one Great Finland and in its great future.

Elias Simojoki was an extremist, who did not wish to know of compromises between right and wrong, strength or weakness. But simultaneously he had the inner humility of a real Christian. These were both attributes he also wished to imprint on the AKS. It is clear that no single individual — not even Simojoki himself — alone made the AKS what it is known as today. But as its founder, he was the author of its main direction: a love for the suffering Finnic population of Eastern Karelia and Ingria, and an uncompromising desire to forward the cause of Greater Finland. Simojoki was glad to see his ideas of a national awakening find success among the very best of the current generation of academic youth. These fighting youth adopted as their idol Bobi Sivén[9] "who preferred to die by his own hand rather than retreat from the position he had himself elected." For everyone who rallied around the AKS flag, the story of his life and death has been explained thus: "be like him, loyal even to death." After a year of activity, AKS was fortunate enough to have as leader the well-known activist Dr. E.E. Kaila. He lit a fiery spirit of patriotism in our young group, as well as a willingness to sacrifice oneself for the greater whole.

Another deep mark in the spirit of the AKS was left by Niilo Kärki, M.A., who personified a clear and courageous desire to heal the rift within our people. As he himself expressed in 1923: "We have awakened from the nightmare of 'red' or 'white' Finns." Other members of AKS — those still with us — introduced Finnish national symbols into the society's fighting program, based on the belief that only a deep national awakening would create a real, triumphant will to greatness among the people. Others went on to include all the fragments of our tribe (not only Karelians or Ingrians), who find themselves outside our national borders, and a striving toward a close collaboration between all of our tribal brethren.

There, different points on the agenda became an organic whole

---

[9] Hans Håkon (H. H.) Christian "Bobi" Sivén was a tribal activist who committed suicide in protest of the Tarto agreement.

and, over the years, a common worldview for an entire generation of militant youth. At the same time, membership grew from hundreds into thousands, and soon enough it took absolute command over all university faculties and student associations, winning over even those young intellectuals who chose not to take the final step of "lifetime conscription," which is what the membership of the AKS truly means. Elias Simojoki felt greatly gratified when following the success of the society he had founded, but he never took on the duty of the leader of the AKS, since he returned to the countryside soon.

However, returning to Helsinki in the 1930s, he belonged to the board of the AKS. Whatever his official position within the organization, he remained its very first member until the end of his life, which made his station within it unique. Many of his speeches were given at AKS events, and these greatly shaped and developed the spirit of the association.

It would have been completely contrary to Simojoki's personality to completely cloister himself in a reading cell during his student years. Nevertheless, he was successful in his studies. In the spring of 1923, he completed his studies in theology and was ordained as a priest the following June. In the fall of 1923, he returned to Helsinki intending to continue his studies, but his plans were interrupted in early 1924, and in April 1924 he entered the military to carry out his mandatory military service. During this brief stay in the capital, he did have time to take part in student politics in a very active manner as the AKS secretary.

Simojoki began his career in the priesthood as an assistant to his own father in Kiuruvesi. As a talented man of the cloth, he would eventually have had the opportunity to pursue a more notable position within the church, but he remained a country priest until the end of his life. As vicar's assistant, he worked for two years in Kiuruvesi, and after that in the country parish of Iisalmi for two years, and a year in the country parish of Kemi. In 1929, he was appointed into the position of minister in Kiuruvesi, a position he held for the rest of his life. He also worked as a teacher of theology in the Kiuruvesi lyceum from September 1929, and this was also a position he held until his death. This was an activity he especially loved, which allowed him to be near youth, who in turn were touchingly devoted to their inspiring teacher.

In the parishes where Simojoki worked as a shepherd of souls, his influence will not soon be forgotten. As a preacher, he was without a doubt among the finest of his generation. His proclamations had a heart-rending, uncompromising quality to them. It was characterized by a wondrous clarity and spiritual strength which broke into the feelings of the audience. During his sermons, the audience felt like he had a message especially for them. Due to his refusal to compromise, Simojoki wished to make sure that everyone knew he was, first and foremost, a *servant* of God and his parish. It never even crossed his mind to merely focus on the absolute minimum of day-to-day matters of the parish. Instead, he was always on the move among his parish, tirelessly traveling back and forth to hold conventicles. He was especially fond of holding them in small cabins in remote villages. He was in the habit of stating that the spirit of God is always closer to modest huts than handsome mansions. And he never hurried away from his congregation, least of all when he was visiting someone who was ill. It has been said that he had something about him that reinforced the better part of every person, which would lead to his recovery. Yet he was also approachable; there was nothing haughty or arrogant about him, but rather despite his ideological inflexibility, he was always friendly and helpful and never tried to hide the fact that he did not consider himself personally an important individual. No person in this congregation ever sought his help in vain. Nor was his help restricted to words, in the form of advice and consolation, but he also helped in deed. His generosity was great. Whatever worldly good he had, it never caused him hardship to share it with those in need. He was an exemplary shepherd for his parish. As such he finally won the hearts of those members who initially were skeptical of him during the years of political turmoil in the 1930s.

When his body was lowered into the grave of the heroic fallen in his home municipality, the entire parish joined together in gratitude and longing, and especially his former opponents desired to join in to show their respect for a man whom they realized they had at first misjudged. When he was gone the people of Kiuruvesi felt like they had lost not just a churchman, but a friend.

Elias Simojoki knew he had found his own place in life in parish work. In a different time, he would no doubt have remained among the country folk he loved so much. But then came the years of interior political crisis, which led him to take a central role in our national struggle. From the countryside, he had followed the developments in our nation closely. The passing years had done nothing to dilute the great dream of his student years. If anything, his conviction deepened that only by going through a deep nationalist awakening and growing the geographical borders of Greater Finland can our nation guarantee its permanent place among free peoples. However, our nation's political life failed to show any indication of development toward greatness. If anything, forces greatly hostile to such goals, forces that tirelessly gnawed at the very foundations of society, grew in influence. Toward the end of the 1920s, it became apparent that we were heading toward a crisis of the greatest severity.

In such circumstances, it was clear to Elias Simojoki that he could not remain outside of the struggle. Instead, he threw himself into it with the same passion and refusal to compromise that characterized his actions in everything else. This led him to Finland's parliament, of which he was a member with the Isänmaallinen Kansallisliike (IKL, the Patriotic People's Movement) from 1933 to 1939. Those were years full of struggle and strife. He took part in parliamentary debates fearlessly and delivered many fiery and memorable speeches from the parliament's podium. Regardless of the storm, his speeches raised every time, he would mercilessly flog all that is low, wrong, and wicked. Later, when considering his career in the parliament as a whole, he admitted that he never failed to maintain a pure and honest mind, and always fought for the correct cause.

But taking into consideration our nation's political life in general during these years, it was obvious that he would become a figure of hate among his opponents. Simojoki himself never considered parliamentary work to be his true calling in life. And without a doubt this assessment was correct. Simojoki was a nationalist awakener, not a political player. And as such many saw him as a perfect target, one toward which they usually shoot their most poisonous arrows. Often his name was dragged through the mud, and his most sincere efforts were deliberately misunderstood. This caused his sensitive mind great suffering. And even this was not enough as he pointed out in one of his speeches to the Blue-Black youth in 1937:

> As long as we are opposed and hated, we will know our course is the correct one. Always walk against the wind; then you will reach your destination. This is what a young soldier did after the battle of Salmijärvi during the Petsamo campaign. He became snow-blind and became separated from his comrades, but he knew that they were in the north, from where the wind was also blowing. In blindness, he crawled through the fells, always feeling the freezing northern wind in his face, until he reached his destination. Lads, always walk toward the wind – crawl, if your strength does not allow you to walk – but always remember: toward the wind.

But as a nationalist leader, he knew full well that such a simplistic solution was not possible for him personally. In the same speech he pointed out:

> The burden carried by a leader of a nationalist youth movement is a heavy one. They must fight not only the outside world, but they must fight many a grueling inner battle within when searching for the proper path for themselves and the youth who follow them.

The most bitter pill of these years was the question burning in his mind: Did he really have the right to lead his comrades and younger followers into the dead end and state of siege, that the powers that be of the time seemed to have condemned them to permanently? All of this led to his bitterness, which is all too apparent in his final political speeches. The years Simojoki spent in Helsinki due to his parliamentary work would have been intolerable for him, if it had not been for the opportunity to work again as a youth leader. In the band of brothers that the AKS had become he met once again the will to fight that had only been strengthened by the opposition it had met over the years. This was, among all the negative trends of the time, a promise for a brighter future. In addition, in 1933 he took over the leadership of Sinimustat (the Blue-Blacks) and later Mustapaidat (the Black Shirts).

Boys and girls from all social classes had joined these organizations. Among these teens Simojoki's position of leadership was uncontested. In his many writings in the organization's magazine, and equally, in his many speeches at the events they organized, he poured the fighting spirit for Greater Finland into his followers. Simojoki's goal with the youth organizations he led was the same he had had in all of his previous political and organizational work.

It was made apparent in the remarks he made, for example, from the podium in the parliament in November 1934:

Our battlefield is the soul of Finland's youth, and we will not cease to fight until we have won a decisive victory. We will not give up until our youth have a strong nationalist and patriotic spirit, which gives our faith the high status it deserves. This work, and the success it achieves, is what the future of Finland depends on… and if there was to be no work toward nationalist awakening done among the youth, then what kind of lads would we then have, at a moment of danger, to show against the youth of Russia, who really are driven by an imperialist zeal?

As a youth leader, Simojoki tirelessly reiterated the need to build on a religious foundation of perfect moral propriety. As he once remarked in a youth rally:

> *Still, we must humbly remember that the perfect nation is not down here. It can only ever be achieved up there, beyond any imperfection. The youth who walk the path guided by their love for the Fatherland must always remember this.*

At the time, his demand that the youth of Finland be militarized was met with incredulous anger. The core of his youth mentorship program was that while it was necessary to equip the military adequately, it was equally necessary to make sure the human material, who would wield these weapons, was adequate. For him, not even the most fervent patriotism and desire for Greater Finland would suffice alone, but he realized the importance of physical fitness as well. He himself was a skillful skier, swimmer, and marksman. And he demanded the same of the youth who followed him:

> *You must learn to march, to swim, to shoot, because the final struggle requires not only the strength of the soul but of the body as well.*

As a shepherd of souls, Simojoki was a friend and helper of the poor, and always wanted to raise the youth to feel similarly. He stressed innumerable times that all of Finland's youth must familiarize themselves with the lives of the working class, learn to think and feel in a *social* manner, and be prepared to fight for true social justice. This was a program, which surely it now must be admitted, that must form the basis for any new, determined youth education.

Elias Simojoki was the founder of AKS and two youth organizations. But he was not an organizer at heart. He was an awakener and inspirer, who drew especially youth toward him, with the clarity of his vision for the future. As a speaker he certainly was remarkable. A certain gentleman of an older generation describes the effect he had on his audience as follows:

> *His proclamation had something of a divine storm and thunder, earthquake and fire, for example when he described the deaths of Ingrian mothers in the Siberian wilderness. But always, in the end, there remained a quiet and gentle wind, the work of the Holy Spirit in a previously cold heart, which the Lord had allowed to return. In many ways, he was a strange apparition here in the cold north. He had the exploding strength of Huguenots, a clarity and holiness of purpose.*

Specifically, Simojoki was a man of the *living* word. Often when he climbed onto the podium, he only had with him an outline of a speech, typically a few sentences long. And even on those occasions when he had prepared his entire speech in advance, he rarely glanced at his notes. He spoke from the heart, and as such his words correspondingly found their way into the hearts of his listeners. His bright eyes commanded the audience to pay attention, and his whole demeanor spoke of such deep conviction that no one was left indifferent.

His voice was not especially deep, and his diction had some room for improvement. Even so, his ability to fascinate the listener was unique. He made his audience laugh and weep with equal ease. In the midst of an oppressive and small-minded historical era, he managed to summon enormous vistas for the future and convinced thousands upon thousands of the possibility of them being within reach. He transferred his burning love for Ingria and Karelia into wide parts of the populace. Few eyes remained dry when he — his voice shaking with internal distress — described the fates of our tribal brethren, who had been exiled from their homesteads. He minced no words when describing the only path he saw for our national salvation:

Finland must either stand or fall with Karelia. The Finnish people must share either glory or ignominy with the Karelians.

If we fail to learn that in order to be great, we must fight, we shall drown.

For us, it is of the utmost importance that one day we shall see the sun rise from behind Karelian forests, free of Russian occupation.

People of Finland: it is you, who must achieve this, and after God, it is in yourself that you must put your faith in.

After all, our goal must not be any less than this: that one day we leave this nation and this people to the following generations even greater and more wonderful than as it was given to us by the generations past.

That moment — the decisive moment of destiny — may arrive at any moment. We can hear the moment of the collapse of Russia coming, as we can hear the wind blowing.

Simojoki was absolutely convinced that as a people we must decide between two mutually exclusive extremes: national greatness, or utter national downfall and destruction. And he saw the decisive moment approaching. Therefore it caused him great pain and distress when he realized with what indifference the political elite regarded the same coming storm and neglected the necessity of preparing for it. It was this that made him speak the following from the parliament podium:

What will this people say to their youth, if they send them off to the fields of death with inadequate weapons? Why are you, the meek fathers of our nation, so concerned over the politicization of our youth, when your concern should be the woeful lack of quality machine guns?

It was this question of national responsibility to our youth that refused him a moment's peace. It was also this matter that led him to propose the occupation of the Karelian Isthmus with voluntary forces. The idea was floating in the very air. In the summer of 1938, the AKS had engaged in a propaganda offensive that covered the entire nation, in which its members held 500 rallies and discussed matters of national defense to over 100,000 people. When assessing the results the following autumn, the idea was brought forward that the following summer, special attention would be paid to the Karelian Isthmus. After all, being unfortified constituted a real Achilles heel in our national defense.

But these plans had no clear and concise form until Elias Simojoki came along in an AKS meeting held on February 22, 1939. He proposed that the organization demand that the government urgently begin constructing fortifications in the Karelian Isthmus and that AKS would provide volunteer workers for this purpose, for the summer of that year. He considered it within the realm of possibility that he could mobilize 100,000 men for this purpose. As is well known, the "shovel Jäger" movement he envisioned became a true populist uprising in the spring of 1939. Their military achievements remained modest, but in terms of morale, their importance was incalculable.

A certain officer, overseeing the construction work, said: "These fortifications have been built by the people of Finland themselves, and the Finnish army will never retreat from them." And when the firestorm on our borders broke a few months later, the entire world would see that this indeed was the case.

When the "non-scheduled refresher training" began the following fall, Elias Simojoki could have stayed home but left for the front without hesitation. Leaving home was as difficult for him as it was for anyone else. He left his young wife and his firstborn child, who had been born the previous spring. Their fate pressed heavily on his mind because he had sensed that this time he would not return.

On the eve of the declaration of war, he was glad to hear that he was being transferred to the position of priest in the regiment to which many other men from Kiuruvesi belonged. He was both a soldier and keeper of souls in this position — in the most demanding conditions imaginable. He took part in every battle with the lads from his home parish and many times risked his own life to rescue a wounded comrade. And at moments of rest, he transformed the tents into conventicles, where the word of God was taught. This last part of his life has been described beautifully:

> *The day he faced the enemy with the men of his home parish for the first time was the hardest for him. The enemy's assault was surprisingly fierce. Men fell and were pulled away. Simojoki went up and down the chain, gave encouragement, looked after the wounded, and told those who had lost their will to advance to instead take the positions left vacant by the attackers. Under heavy fire, he dragged a wounded commanding officer to a field hospital. At all times he moved on the battlefield as if he himself was safe and it was only everyone else who was in mortal danger. He forgot himself and devoted himself to his comrades in arms. After receiving this harsh baptism of fire, and returning to their tents at night, the other side of Elias Simojoki's character was revealed. Forty men of Kiurujoki had fallen or gone missing, and Simojoki cried, cried out loud. His heart was at its breaking point that night. A piece of his beloved Karelia had been lost, even though it had been soaked in the blood of his own countrymen.*

Elias Simojoki did not live to see the happier turn of that decisive battle. An enemy bullet pierced his head on January 25, 1940. He fell on the ice covering Lake Ladoga at a time when the grim outcome of the Winter War was becoming apparent.

No one knows what he felt and thought during his final days. Perhaps he was pained by the idea that he would not be present when the Finnish army would make his fondest dream a reality by marching into Olonets and the White Sea Karelia. But without a doubt he saw further, beyond the bitterness of defeat, to a day of victory in the future. It was with profound joy that he witnessed the miracle of national unity that was autumn 1939 for our people, which became a source of strength to carry them through all difficulty to a bright future. It was with this knowledge that he found it easy to believe at least in the awakened will to the greatness of our people. After all, he had never ceased to believe it even in the darkest years of division and internal strife. In life, Elias Simojoki was not a particularly well-known or recognized public figure. He was a pathfinder with a clear vision for the future. His words lead us, on the winding path of our people, from the weakness and confusion of the 1920s to the "promised land." In a speech he gave in 1922 he spoke:

> *That great, all-encompassing, all-conquering love of the Fatherland is the burning bush from which the God of nations speaks to his subjects.*

In this sense, Simojoki himself was a burning bush for the people of Finland. And the day will yet come when he is recognized as a national hero in Finland, the country he loved so passionately, and for which he gave everything.

Elias Simojoki (1899–1940)

Do You Remember?

Suomen Heimo (*Finland's Tribe*) **Magazine Issue 8/1923**

You ask me, brother, how is it that I still find the strength to toil and work here for the good of Karelia. You mock me and our spiritual struggle. Furthermore, you do not consider a war that is fought with the brain and with the heart to be a true war. But rather, only a war that is fought with gunpowder and steel. You also ask, how does it feel to fight with the pen and the word, for a man who in the past had the joy of pressing a rifle against his cheek in the endless woods of Karelia, and you ask: Do you remember?

Brother from years gone by! I do still remember, and that is precisely why I still fight. You scorn the spiritual war. My answer to you is: so did I in the past, but no longer, for I now know what a spiritual war may mean for the spirit and the body. I know how much bravery was needed in the wars of Finland and Karelia in the past, but even more so do we need it now, for the war that we now find ourselves in. I know how badly in the past we needed loyalty, but even more so do we need it now. We needed perseverance and willingness, but now we need it much, much more.

In this war, you will not see the enemy felled by a bullet, but still, you must believe. In this war, your hand will not grip the flagpole of a defeated enemy, but you must have the strength to hope. In this war, your starving comrade will not share his last crust of bread with you, nor will he shelter you from the cold with the helm of his own coat, and yet, you must have the strength to love him all the same. In this war, your enemy is not the neighboring tribe, but it may very well be your very own brother or sister. In this war, your blood will not be spilled by the enemy's steel, but it will burn and scour your heart for as long as it beats.

I do not know if you understand me. I do not know if you follow my meaning when I say that I continue to struggle precisely *because* I remember. And I wish to ask you the same question that you asked me: Do you remember when young blood was spilled in the wilderness of the White Sea and Olonets, in vain as it seemed, and yet we were prepared to give our blood nevertheless?

Do you remember how in the year 1918 in Vuokkiniemi[10], your fingers tried in vain to stop the blood gushing from a comrade's wounds, and how he told us to leave on his own devices because the battle was still unfinished? Do you remember how our nostrils gorged themselves on the smell of gunpowder and our hearts pounded with the joy of battle when we rushed through the Russians' barbed-wire fences into Tuulos[11] in 1919? Do you remember the rush of victory above their trenches, because we had vanquished an enemy that outnumbered us by 10? Do you remember how we found hanging, from those same barbed wires, a lad from Ostrobothnia … of only 13 years? Do you remember how we were forced to board a ship bound for Finland in Vitele?[12] Do you remember what von Hertzen[13] told that band of stragglers, once awesome in their strength? Do you remember how we then cried, each of us alone in secret? Do you remember how the winter before last we abandoned a village paid for in blood to the Russians? Do you remember how the poor Karelians hugged our knees, begging us to stay? Do you remember the starved and frozen heroes and the half-naked women and children collapsing in the snows of Karelia, as a crushed army and

---

[10] Vuokkiniemi: In Russian: Voknavolok, a town in Karelia.
[11] Tuulos is an area in the Tavastia region of Finland. Heavy fighting took place here during the Finnish civil war of 1918.
[12] Vitele is a town in the Olonets district in Karelia
[13] Gunnar von Hertzen (1893–1973) was an officer in the Finnish Jäger Battallion

a crushed people walked their Via Dolorosa toward Finland?

You do remember. I know you remember; we both remember this and much, much more, even though at times we might wish to forget. I know you now understand why I still fight. I know that now not only do you understand, but you will join me in the same front and the same struggle.

Finland's Dawn

AKS Independence Day Ceremony
Finland's National Theater, December 6, 1922

Unhappy are the bloodied, robbed, mutilated, raped, shackled land and people of Karelia! Unhappy, the entire shattered tribe of Finland, the happiest part of whom still live in a free, albeit constantly threatened country! Unhappy tribe, condemned by history to wage an endless struggle against the vast ocean of Slavic tribes. A large part of our tribe has already drowned in it.

Where are the legendary braves of Bjarmaland?[14] The voices of the Voguls[15] have gone silent, the Votes[16] equally. Apparently now it has been decreed that it is the turn of our people's most vulnerable and most talented tribe, the Karelians, the creators of the *Kalevala*,[17] to be destroyed. For now, we still hear their pleas for help, but soon they too shall be silenced like Bjarmians or Voguls of old. We are hearing the final agonies of our brethren. Most of the people of Karelia walk a miserable road as refugees, and those who remain in their own lands face a fate that will shake even a heart of stone.

When the struggle for the survival of our brother tribe is in such a critical stage, with the enemy using the type of language we have become accustomed to recently, it seems weaker than

---

[14] Bjarmaland is an area south of the White Sea. The Bjarmians have been extinct since at least the 13th Century. They are often confused with the Permians, another Finno-Ugric tribe.
[15] Voguls are a Finno-Ugric people today referred to as the Mansi. Their homeland is in the Khanty-Mansia region in Western Siberia.
[16] Votes are the indigenous people of Votia, a part of Ingria.
[17] Finland's national epic, compiled by Elias Lönnrot in several expeditions into Karelia and first published in 1835

weak to strike with words, when we should strike with steel. When Russians reply with actual genocidal raids, as the papers have told us, a speech given from a podium seems like a hopelessly weak response. We Finns, who for a long time have had the questionable privilege of having close dealings with the Russians, know full well what these "punishment raids" actually are. We know they leave blood and smoking ruins in their wake, and our hearts shake. For some, it is with horror, for others with pity, yet others with hatred.

Again the time has come when the Finn and the Karelian who love their Fatherland hopelessly look around them with (if this is even possible) even more bitter despair, wondering if there is any direction from which rescue might still arrive. He looks around as before, and looks in vain as before, for wherever it may be that he looks, in the halls of great nations or within our broken ranks, it looks just as dark and hopeless. The rescue fails to come, and it is becoming late, for if it does not arrive soon, the Karelian people will be lost, and once again another branch of our once so proud tribal tree will be severed. The ax has already been placed under the tree in Karelia, and many times already, in fact, it has struck its side and will soon strike through into its very heart. And yet, what makes the pain this causes all the more unbearable, is the sad observation that becomes more obvious day by day and year by year, that the Finnish people are not *awake*.

What has caused our people to fall asleep? What created its slave mentality? Did not the Finnish Lion awaken, when it cast off the slave's yoke, or did it not fully understand that its work was left badly unfinished? Did not the blood sacrifice that the freedom required remove the slave's mind for good and replace it with a new spirit and mind, one that is essential for every free people who strive for greatness? It has to be said that unfortunately, it does not seem to be so. The millennia of slavery our people have had to suffer under — at times under the Slavic, at times under the Germanic peoples — has left its mark and remains even after the joyful spring of our freedom. There is still a drop of slave's blood in our veins. After all, if it were not so, if the Finnish people felt their freedom, like someone truly free feels it — joyful, triumphant, as an all-conquering and all-sacrificing force — would we really allow the enemy to rape the Karelian land, which embraces our own country and in fact is an integral part of it? Would our people deign to beg for scraps from the tables of the rich, in a way no one who is truly free would dream of doing? And what if we were to trust our own strength? Would we not grab the reins from the hands of our enemies, whether these enemies are internal or foreign? Would we not cease to squander our tremendous strength in squabbling among ourselves, as we are doing now? Do we not dare to dream of greatness?

Did someone recoil? Did someone sense a whiff of the controversial idea of Greater Finland? It is precisely what I am getting at, even if this idea is considered dead, defeated, an illusion, a product of a fanatic, feverish brain with no basis in reality or realistic hopes of it being achieved. What else is it proof of, than of a slave mentality, when a people cannot even dream of the greatness of which they are actually fully deserving? Where else, if not from our long historical path full of foreign hegemony and the enslavement of our own people, can the idea have its origin, that our people's hearts must be stripped of all dreams of greatness? If it weren't for the greatest men of our people, daring to believe in our freedom century after century, where would our freedom be now? That hope, claimed by many to be madness and illusions, dragged through the mud by others, came true at a moment when it seemed to be further than ever. Our people are not yet fully awake, as a nation. They still walk tethered by foreigners. They remain blindfolded, with no understanding of what to speak, how to act, what to fight for. They swing blindly left and right, attacking even those who are flesh of their flesh and blood of their blood and who often represent precisely those among us who have brought about the happiest outcomes in our history. In their blindness, they attack those who still carry a spark of love that suffers all, survives all, and finally conquers all, those whose dream is to lift their own nation to glory and greatness, so that it will include all of our tribes and our true geographical area. The Finnish people must wake up to this awareness. We have the right, and not only the right, the *duty* to include within our nation the tribes and lands that undoubtedly belong to us. Our historical role as a guarding wall against the East is too serious to neglect, and we would be failing our duty to the West if we do not make the Karelian cause our own and carry it to a happy conclusion. This is our task for humanitarian and national reasons alone. Besides, if we fail to stand up and fight for our own greatness, we will vanish just like innumerable other peoples before. We shall be forgotten; we shall be erased from the pages of history, the same pages on which the Shepherd of Nations has given us an opportunity to write our names in indelible letters. And along with us, many other Western people may vanish as well. Every nation and people that have become great and powerful, has begun by daring to dream of its own greatness and to elevate themselves above others in their national price and self-esteem. Such a people become the favorite child of history. Their faith in themselves carries them forward, even through seemingly impossible obstacles and difficulties. Such a people are not bound by regular laws of nature; they defy the logic of what is possible and what is not. They create miracles instead and if necessary, defy the entire world with them.

Nevertheless, if any people truly have the seed of greatness within them, it is ours. We have shown it with achievements only the great are capable of. History has given us a task, one I mentioned just now, a task so high and great, that to merely think of it boggles the mind: the task of defending the entire civilized world from the imperialist raids of barbarians. To whom History hands out mighty tasks, she also gives the tools required to perform them. These are most certainly not lacking in our people. I do not speak of our people's accomplishments in modern civilized life. I prefer to talk of the miracles we have performed elsewhere.

What infinity of mental capital, physical strength, endurance, tenacity, and bravery that fearlessly shatters everything in its path has been condensed into our small nation! Have not these people, familiar with frost and bark bread, the people of Saarijärven Paavo,[18] shown their tenacity when they cleared fields here in the cold north, now covered with golden wheat? Are we not the same people, who mock death and rush to battle as the Hackpells[19] did, whose spears stopped the enemy attacks on the battlefields of Breitenfeld and Lützen! Does not our recent history remind us that the same spirit lives on in our sons? It was not extinguished after the Great Northern War. Where once were Breitenfeld, Lützen, and Hackpells, we now have Eckau-Keckau, Misse and Aa, and the Jägers. Tales of Narva, the men of Charles XII, have come back to life, in the form of the Finnish heroes of the Estonian War of Independence of 1919, many of whom are still with us or have been laid to rest only a few short years ago. Do we not remember Ensign Stål,[20] of whom Runeberg[21] sang? Do not the monuments erected to honor the heroic dead, which adorn almost every one of our churchyards, speak a language that is alive enough for you?

There are quiet funeral mounds everywhere between the Kola Peninsula and the shores of river Svir, who speak their own mute language and tell us of new guerrilla warriors who followed the path of Vesainen and Löfving,[22] who grew pale only in death. If only the old trees in the old battlefields, where once again Finnish blood was spilled in recent years, could speak, imagine what they would say. Much of it we know, but also much of it has been forgotten, for the men who suffered through all of it, belong to the

---

[18] Saarijärven Paavo, is the titular character in a poem by Runeberg, a farmer who suffers hardship.

[19] Hackpells were Finnish light cavalryman in the service of King Gustavus Adolphus of Sweden.

[20] The Tales of Ensign Stål is an epic by Runeberg which describes the Finnish War of 1808-09.

[21] Johan Ludvig Runeberg, 1804 – 1877 Finland's national poet and author of Finland's national anthem.

[22] Pekka Vesainen (1540-1627) and Stefan (Tapani) Löfving (1689-1777) were Finnish guerrilla chiefs who fought against Russian occupation, the first one during the "long wrath" of 1570–1595, the second during the "great wrath" of 1700-1721.

silent[23] of the land, who wished no glory for themselves, and their heroism had no other witnesses than distant wilderness and woods.

We know our people still possess this quiet, hidden strength. We know we still have the same bravery, the same daring and endurance, and true greatness. Dare we not then believe, that if only our people themselves were to realize this, the time of Finland's greatness would come at long last! It shall happen; it is merely waiting for the right psychological moment to burst forward, the great dawn of awakening that shall remake all. Sakari Topelius[24] writes that no amount of men can thaw a frozen lake, no matter how hard they beat it with iron bars or shovels, but once the sun shines on its surface at the right moment, soon the wintry ice melts and the summery waves return. It is that opportune moment, free from all contraption and artificiality, that our people wait for, and they wait for the fulfillment of their rightful wishes. This moment will come as long as we have the strength to believe, to hope, and to love. Then the binds will come apart as if by magic; the ice in our hearts will melt; the time for springtime miracles will have arrived. Believing in that moment, even a mind mired in depression dares to glow, to burn.

May that hope grow great and powerful, majestic; may the knees of the people bend before it! May our people's hearts be filled with a love for the Fatherland that is so strong, so bright that it ignites even embers that have been cold for so long. May its burning be such that it refuses to grant peace even in sleep, but rather compels one to work and to do battle for as long as the work is still unfinished. That great, all-encompassing, all-conquering love of the Fatherland is the burning bush from which the God of nations speaks to his subjects, and it is with the help of such a God that a newly awakened people in the spring of their first love perform their miracles. The blood spilled in the Karelian

---

[23] The Finnish Bible says that it is the silent, rather than the meek, who shall inherit the land.
[24] Zachris (Zacharias, Sakari) Topelius (1818 –1898), author, poet, journalist, historian, and rector of the University of Helsinki.

wilderness in three years was not in vain. The suffering was not without purpose. The great God of nations looks fondly on a sacrifice made for a proper cause. When freedom for Karelia finally comes, it shall be seen that after all, that blood sacrifice was one of the factors that prepared for it. When the historical moment arrives for our people, the liberation of Karelia is a mere detail in our history of greatness. The vigil fires in Karelia will be lit again as if by themselves; our people will rise up and charge the enemy side by side with our tribal brothers and show that we still know how to fight, even to die if necessary, but also to *triumph*. Tshirkka-Kemi[25] and Svir, the shores of Onega[26] and Ladoga, and Karelia shall be free — and then, *then* Finland's dawn will come.

---

[25] Thsirkka-Kemi is a river in Karelia
[26] Onega (Finnish *Ääninen*) is a lake in Karelia, the second-largest lake in Europe. It is to the east of Ladoga, which is Europe's largest lake.

I Believe in the Coming Greatness of Finland

Speech for the Fatherland at the Annual Gala of the
Northern Ostrobothnian Student Nation,[27] February 5, 1923

May the patriotic citizen be forgiven, that when he wishes to speak to his country, the country he speaks to is Greater Finland. That when he wishes to speak to his people, the people he speaks to are the people of Greater Finland.

One may ask, does he really have that right, for the people of Finland have always been small, and remain so today. But presently the view among nationalist citizens is that the concepts of Fatherland and Greater Fatherland are the same, and thus when the citizen addresses his nation, he speaks to them as a great nation, speaks to his people as a great people. Besides, the greatness of a people is not a numerical issue. It is decided by the achievements and values of that same people. It can be said, that despite being small, this people has achieved greatness in deeds, for having the strength to stand against Novgorod, Moscow, and then St. Petersburg for a millennium. Finland was great when we fought under the Swedish flag in Denmark, Poland, Russia, and Germany — even if this greatness has not been mentioned in the pages of world history.

We struck our mark on our own country and under the proud colors of Sweden. The famed Black Regiment[28] was wiped out to the last man twice, once in the Russian war, then again in the Danish war. It was the Finnish battle-axe that breached the walls

---

[27] Student nations are associations of university students based on their geographical home regions.

[28] The Black Regiment was a dragoon regiment drafted from eastern Finland in 1665.

of Novgorod and Warsaw. The first swords to flash atop the walls of Narva were those of Finns. The walls of Vienna shook as the Finnish dragoons approached. It was when the cries of "hakkaa päälle!"[29] rang out that the ranks of the Croats fell.

Finland has been great on the battlefields of Europe, greater still in times of peace. History has set us down in an inhospitable land, eaten by permafrost, placed a gigantic mortal enemy next to us, gave us a loaf of bark bread in one hand, a mattock in the other and said, "Be fruitful and *multiply!*" And thus the wilderness and swampland gave way to the farms. The man of Finland was great on the battlefields of Europe, but even greater on his own land, when left to his own devices. When the best of us fought for the glory of Sweden in foreign lands, the cripples, the children, and the elderly had to do battle for their own homesteads. The Russians burnt the lands many times over; hunger, plague and the sword were constant visitors, but the seed of the people always survived in hidden cabins in the woods. A new people came forth again and again, always stronger than before. They rose from ashes and blood, built new homes on the ruins, with ax in one hand and a spear in the other, planted new crops, and added tree bark to the baker's dough when necessary.

The people of Finland have never been as great as after the storm of the "Great Hatred,"[30] when we were but 300,000, and we have never been as small as now, though we number three and a half million. We have been this small only in the years of tribal warfare, when Tavastia fought against Savonia, when the Ostrobothnians followed the signal fires to the White Sea, and when revenge raids followed one after the other in both directions. Now, class warfare is even more bitter than the tribal wars of old, the revenge raids more brutal. And yet we see signs of a national awakening; there is a sense of spring approaching.

---

[29] "Hakkaa päälle" is the battle cry of the Hackpells. It is usually translated as "cut them down."

[30] "The Great Hatred" is the Russian occupation of Finland (1700–1721) during the Great Northern War.

Remember the heroic Jägers in Germany and Livonia; remember the historic creation of the white heroes: Finland's freedom.

Remember the glorious battlefields of Estonia and the sign of our tribes uniting. Despite ending in defeat, the uprisings in Karelia and Ingria were also signs of national awakening. The people of Karelia and Ingria extended their hand to us in brotherhood. In three years, Finns fought with our tribal brothers, partook in the glory of victory and the bitterness of defeat. The shards of the Sampo[31] are looking for each other, as we are not used to quitting at the first difficulty. The way to decisive victories has always been through defeat. Tribes uniting has always been a sign of something great being afoot, in the history of nations. This is why we can address our Fatherland and people as great.

Citizens! One of the most joyful and clear signs of Finland's awakening is the wonderful patriotic love now growing among our students. Wonderful, because it combines the love for the Fatherland with a love for our tribal brethren, a love that is tender and faithful. They have realized that the fate of our kindred tribes is also the fate of our fatherland. We know that the greatness this youth strive for is *worldly* greatness. It is a matter of raising our fatherland to the status of a great power. We know that this is our right. We know we are entitled to the lands inhabited by our tribes. We know that our nation has the duty to become great because otherwise, we cannot fulfill our mission as a protective shield for the Western nations against the East. We cannot maintain our present independence within our present borders — if we stay where we are, the Russians' warpath will go over our own graves toward the West. The people of Finland are the last line of defense for the entire civilized world, and woe betides them if our guard fires were to go out! Understanding this, our awakened people work for the Greater Fatherland.

But to reach external greatness, it is necessary to grow into it from within. For external greatness, we must achieve internal

---

[31] The Sampo was a magical artifact in Finland's national epic *Kalevala* that gives good fortune and wealth for its owner. In the end it is destroyed, and its pieces lost in the bottom of the sea.

greatness first. The first prerequisite of this is internal moral strength. We need a sense of being history's chosen people, a sense of calling. Above all, however, we need love. Love for the Fatherland is the bright cloud that has sheltered our people during our millennium of wandering in the desert. Love for the Fatherland, combined with moral self-discipline has been carried out through war and peace and has allowed us to perform feats of greatness. Love for the Fatherland follows the same laws as other forms of love, for it has the same source: God. It is not selfish. It never despairs. It never ceases to believe. It teaches us to live and die for the Fatherland. It never hesitates. Toil and suffering for the sake of the Fatherland are our joy and glory; to die for the Fatherland is to receive the brightest crown. Our youth know how to die for this country. The names on the marble boards in this very hall are proof enough of that. But now we ask our youth to do even more than to die for the Fatherland: we ask them to live for the Fatherland. And it seems that they are doing just that. However, their attempts are without roots and even their greatest achievements will be for nothing unless they return to the God of our forefathers and thus to moral values. In God, our ancestors had their unshakable foundation. He will lead our people to external greatness, via first achieving greatness within. It is He who can instill into the hearts of our nation's prodigal sons a burning love for our Fatherland. Even if we retreated under Klingspor,[32] we will again take our stand on the ice of the Siikajoki River as we did with von Hertzen[33] and create proud traditions again, this time for our own colors rather than the Swedish ones. Finland will certainly wage great wars once again. If we depart for battle in the same spirit as our ancestors did; we shall make our country into a great power, we will extinguish the fires of the Russians in the Land of Heroes and on the banks of the Neva. We

---

[32] Wilhelm Mauritz Klingspor (1744 – 1814) Field Marshal of Finland during the Finnish war of 1808-09.

[33] Ernst Gustav von Hertzen (1765 – 1834 Ruotsinpyhtää) was a Finnish officer during the Finnish war of 1808-09. Not to be confused with the Jäger officer Gunnar von Hertzen previously mentioned.

shall remove the stains of insult in our national honor.

Citizens! Let the goal of the entire Finnic tribe be nothing less than greatness. Our brothers on the Pannonian Steppe, the noble Magyars, vow daily: "I believe in the coming greatness of Hungary." May the rallying cry for every Finn who loves his Fatherland, the only one possible for a free Finland, be: "I believe in the coming greatness of Finland."

Our Will

AKS Flag Dedication Ceremony, May 12, 1923

We wish to sacrifice to You in our hearts, Lord, and pray for you to bless our new flag. May You bless it, for we wish to use it for the purposes of justice and love. If You are with us, then who can stand against us? Bless these lads, who now and in the times to come swear to work for the greatness of their Fatherland, the assistance and liberation of our oppressed tribal brethren, and the downfall of the oppressor people. We do not seek glory for ourselves but wish to restore the honor of our people and Fatherland. We do not seek benefit for ourselves, but rather we wish to suffer and sacrifice, if necessary to spill our heart's blood, so that the shattered tribe of Finland may awake and be restored, the Greater Finnish Fatherland be created as righteousness demands.

Citizens, brothers! Before the Almighty, we have dedicated our black flag, and now we swear loyalty to it. May that loyalty be as true and lasting as only the loyalty of a Finn can be. May our flag remain spotless and its traditions noble, its reputation honorable from the very beginning. May it be always seen where masculine vigor and honor perform miracles.

Our flag is black as night, but after all, it is in the dark night that the shards of our tribe wander; it is still in darkness that we await the fulfillment of our great patriotic dream. But the sword of our faith and hatred strikes bright sparks in the darkness, predicting dawn.

Equally, black is our hatred toward that nation, whose name I shall not mention and by doing so soil this sacred moment. Our hate is as black as this flag, but it is righteous and justified and is driven by the blue and white colors of our love. May this flag symbolize not only our own faith but that of our entire tribe and nation. May a dying eye be brightened by seeing it. Let anyone who is tired raise their eyes toward it and find new strength. Let he who has lost hope see it and find it again.

We salute you, the flag of our love, the flag of our hate and of our desire to sacrifice, the black flag of the Academic Karelia Association. We believe you to be among the clearest signs of our national awakening and tribal resurrection, and we are convinced that we shall see you flying, glorious and immaculate, where the people of Finland perform great works, where our Fatherland's bright future is created, a future that is as bright as this flag is black.

The Revolution in the Hearts of Our People

1923

The argument over direction and purpose that is currently ongoing among Finnish university students is merely a minor squabble if compared with what is to come.

The argument suggests our coming national awakening, which must be spread from students to the entire Finnish people. For the position we represent, it is already a victory that the argument itself is taking place. It is a battle that we would have spreading throughout the entire populace like wildfire. Our declaration of rebellion was a challenge to all of Finland: Greater Finland will be our realm.

The struggle began when we boldly accused our entire people to their face: you remain asleep, you have no national identity, you are not truly independent, you have the mentality of a slave, and if you do not awaken, you shall drown!

Thus, the battle. Now attacks are being made for and against. New factions are being created. New terms and ideas are being argued over. Citizens are being asked — by the Fatherland itself — *what is the truth?* The very existence of this struggle seems to us like an indication of an approaching final victory.

We rejoice because we know that for there to be a victory, there must be a battle. The battle suggests that something of importance is taking place. In a battle, rust will be shaken off old weapons. In the heat of battle, decisions must be made quickly. That which is worthless is quickly discarded, and what is valuable will be held in higher regard than ever. The battle shows what is truly lasting and enduring, and correspondingly, what is best forgotten. It is this battle in which we have taken part in our hearts during sleepless nights and during busy days. We have experienced the rush of victory and the quiet satisfaction of having made our own personal resolutions and decisions. This is why we feel joy when we manage to pull others into the maelstrom and to the path of the struggle we have ourselves walked before, and continue to walk today. For us it has meant old attitudes being abandoned, broken shackles of old opinions and national preconceptions. The results have been a renewed sense of conscience, a new appraisal of old values, old plans, and hopes replaced by new, shining vistas. We also hold the hope that the same internal struggle for a solution would ignite within every citizen. It is up to every individual to decide what their own decision will be.

But in our view, a citizen is not a citizen at all if he fails to independently decide for himself what the truth is. What is it then, that we Finnish students wish to accomplish, to be? We wish to *expand*, not merely preserve, the land our forefathers, those tough pioneers and famed warriors, now rest under. For this task, we wish to engage the entire nation. And even more! We live in the present. We wish to be the nagging conscience of our nation. At a time when the people seem to be forgetting the tragedies of three years of war, across the border among the people of Karelia and Ingria, we wish to remind them, drag off the blindfold applied to our national conscience, to mercilessly accuse them.

The Finnish people shall not be allowed to forget that they are to blame for a shameful, shocking tragedy that fell upon one of their tribes. They must be reminded of their own inaction when their sons bled into the sand in the distant wilderness like a sacrificial calf. They must realize how blind and deaf they were before the prayers of the lads forgotten behind enemy lines. They will not be allowed to forget that when an entire freedom-loving tribe trusted them and waited for their aid, and when that trust was betrayed and this tribe doomed to destruction, there was not a curse spoken from their lips or a single call for the effeminate Finnish people to meet the same fate. When our people seem to wish to wash their blood off their hands, all we want is to yell at them from the wilderness: "It is your brethren's blood that calls to you from the earth!"

We know quite well that the moans we now hear from the pale lips of the defeated peoples of Karelia and Ingria are nothing but a weak echo of all the suffering and tragedies from the millennia of war between Russia and the Finnic peoples. But the tragedy of Karelia of the winter before last *must not be* the last chapter, but rather let there be one final, even more terrifying chapter as a conclusion: the downfall of the Russian people, of the other party. This is not imperialism; it is a battle against imperialism. This is not revenge; it is righteousness.

The millennia of wandering in the wilderness for our once so great and mighty tribe has been dark and bloody, rich only in loss and defeat. Against such a historical background it may seem like madness to talk of its great mission and future, as we do. Still, we do so, for we believe that history does not follow mathematical laws, but rather it bends to a higher will: the will of righteous God, before whom each nation must tremble and bend the knee. Above anything else, our people need to believe in that God and secondly believe in themselves. This belief must transcend belief in the forum of the League of Nations and interim peace agreements. Our people must understand their role in the history of all human development. They need the love that makes work for the Fatherland and suffering for it a shining crown. Each citizen must understand with awe, their tremendous personal responsibility for the fate of the nation, and each one of us must take part in carrying upon our own shoulders the cross that has been placed on the back of our people. This is the path of growth, growth for the individual and the people, growth toward a moral internal greatness, and it is everyone's duty to work toward this — it is all this that we call *nationalist awakening*.

We will deny our people internal peace, as it has been denied us. We will replace it with such fire that gives no peace, day or night, but drives to work, to struggle, for as long as there is work to be done and the battle still rages. It is our hope that we will see our people's national esteem awaken. We wish to see them stand up, shed their beggar's rags, which have been worn to almost nothing, and instead dress themselves in the purple cloak of national pride and gird it with the belt of national self-esteem.

Then their old song "we are content to be small" will be forgotten. Then the old love, which is nothing but a resounding gong or a clanging cymbal, will end. Then they will understand, that they had no real understanding of faith, and no real hope had ever entered their hearts before. Only then will they clearly understand that the Fatherland, as they had previously understood it, is merely a part of it and that the people they had believed made up the nation, was a mere shadow of it. A revolution in the hearts of our people – this is what we prepare for; this is what we believe in. It is a staggeringly high goal; next to it perhaps even such goals as Greater Finland and a free Karelia and Ingria may be secondary. We believe that only the great national awakening may signify hope of victory in this great marathon in which we are taking part, minute after minute, and furthermore, on the moment of such an awakening, the dreams of Greater Finland and freedom for the Finnish tribe will come to pass, as if by themselves.

This is the objective we rush toward, and we have no time to watch out for those who may be trampled underfoot. In the coming battle, we wish nothing for ourselves. We are happy to become insignificant if the Fatherland can become great. We will gladly be poor if the Fatherland is to become rich. We are glad to accept shame and humiliation if the Fatherland's path to glory and honor must pass through our degradation. We will fall into the dust for the nation to use us as a stepping stone if this allows it to ascend higher. The only treasure we desire is the one that rewards our sacrifice and poverty in ways invisible to others. This is the treasure the Fatherland itself offers to us, and therefore we offer ourselves to the Fatherland in turn. The Holy Book says this treasure is the greatest of all: love.

If we are considered madmen and the curved horn of

judgment is blown at us, so be it. We refuse the judgment of the present and continue our work and our battle; the only judgments we accept are those of the future generations. We call the present generation only as witnesses. Let future generations have the privilege of placing us in the seat of either the accuser or the accused.

Peace Upon the Earth

Military Gala, Winter 1924

Christmas — the midwinter celebration — that we are now preparing for, allows even a soldier a moment's respite from the requirements of military service and the strict routines of life in the barracks.

He has the opportunity to take a moment to consider the importance of the event we are now approaching. He remembers the busy preparation for a great feast at home, his mother's hurried preparations in the kitchen, the wide-eyed wonder of his smaller brothers and sisters. He also remembers the clear, starry sky of Christmas night, and the jingling of bells in the darkness, as the family made their way on a sled toward a church lit by hundreds of candles. The people of Finland prepare to celebrate Christmas, to celebrate peace, thinking of the song of angels on the first Christmas night: "Peace on Earth, goodwill to men."

But the Finnish citizen — least of all a Finnish solder — must not forget that while we celebrate the night of peace, the very opposite of peace lurks beyond our borders. The Finn who celebrates Christmas should remember that our people have neighbors of our flesh and blood for whom Christmas has not come in many years. By this, I mean primarily the peoples of Karelia and Ingria. We do not hear the gentle Christmas hymns from Karelia or Ingria. What we hear are the final groans of a dying people. Our tribal brother's homes are in flames, and continuous lamentations can be heard from their *kantele*.[34] The Ingrians' fields are being dug open to be used as Russians' trenches, whose border guards

---

[34] A kantele is a Karelian folk instrument, similar to a zither or a psaltery.

now warm their hands with the embers of their burnt homes. Christmas is dreadful in Karelia, equally dreadful and devoid of joy in the formerly so delightful Ingrians' land. It seems clear that the Russian has decided to combine all his forces to carry out the final act of the millennia-long tragedy of the Finnic tribe. They are preparing to destroy its most noble part, Karelia, and therefore they threaten all of Finland along with it.

Soldiers! See, Christmas is here, but once more the sky to the southeast is red, and dark storm clouds spread to our skies. I spoke of a tragedy for the entire Finnic tribe, intentionally. Think of all that history has had to do, in order to shatter this land and people into such a degraded state. Once the same tribe numbered in the tens of millions. As reminders of the series of catastrophes that our tribe has had to endure during our thousand years in the wilderness, we have Moscow, built on the land of the Meryans,[35] Archangel in Bjarmaland, and the stone city of St. Petersburg, built on the Ingrians' homeland. The voices of the Voguls have gone silent; the Votes are gone. They have been smothered by the monstrous embrace of Russia.

Think of the shocking stories of the desperate battles the Finnic tribes have fought in their former homesteads, before they vanished, bloodied in defeat, into gigantic Russia. History is as mute before these facts as the endless prairies of Siberia. It is nevertheless a fact that our lands once extended to Lake Baikal. The battle between the Finnic tribe and Russians has raged over a thousand years, and our defeats have been crushing. The war has raged on, until the very recent past, and we only have a few victories to our name: the freedom of Finland and Estonia.

However, the defeats in Karelia, in three years of war, in 1918, 1919, and 1921, have been significant. Silent funerary mounds from the White Sea to the banks of the Svir tell us of the heroes who did not hesitate to spill their blood alongside the finest sons of Karelia. Our boys have bled, in that vast wilderness, as if they

---

[35] The Meryans are an extinct Finno-Ugric tribe.

were sacrificial lambs.

Why do I remind you of these painful events during a Christmas feast? I wish to reiterate the mission that we, as Finnish soldiers, must never forget. We must not, even at Christmastime, allow ourselves to forget, that things are not yet as they must be. We have a valuable inheritance to claim in the land in which our forefathers' bones are buried. We must learn to continuously work toward doing this and be prepared to sacrifice ourselves for it.

Equally, we must learn to recognize our duty to liberate the people of Karelia from Eastern slavery. It is our duty to create a free Fatherland for tribal brethren, a free and great Fatherland for our descendants. This great work must be carried out, even if it were to deprive us of peace during the day and of restful sleep at night. Carrying out this task should be our passion, one that fills our every thought, and gives us a burning desire to sacrifice our very life if necessary.

If we neglect this task, if we do not drive the Russian out of our great Fatherland, there will never be a true Christmas for our people, there will be no peace upon the land and no good will among its people. This task is massive and our responsibility before it feels mighty. But why should we fail to achieve it? We are the people who produced the Hackpells, whose spears broke the enemy. We are the juniper people,[36] familiar with cold and hunger, who have overcome the Russians' attacks century after century, without breaking. We have raised our sword in the Great Northern War, during the Finnish war of 1808-09, and our Freedom war. And at times of great anguish, we have raised our eyes and looked to the future with faith and hope.

Soldiers of Finland! Let us learn to trust in nothing but God and ourselves! Whether we wish it or not, we approach minute by minute the great battle, where it will be decided whether the name of our tribe is erased from the book of nations for good or if a new

---

[36] Finns sometimes refer to themselves as "the juniper people," since a juniper tree will not break even if bent.

page, the most glorious of all, is written. When that moment arrives, it will be seen if we measure up to that proud designation: "a Finnish soldier."

Let us pray that we shall prove ourselves worthy, so that we may leave our land and people to the future generations even greater and more lovely than the previous generations gave it to us. And if those times are to prove full of hardship, let us remind ourselves of what Saarijärven Paavo had to say for himself: "The Lord gives and takes away, but He never abandons." And let it be so, that one day, perhaps not in our lifetimes, but one day, the sun shall rise from behind the hills of a Karelia free of Russians. And then shall there be peace upon the land and goodwill among men.

Finland Has Not Yet Been – Finland Is Still to Come

Tribal Rally in Kuopio April 7, 1925

We hold our tribal celebration at a time when it is utterly quiet in Karelia when the whole issue appears to be at a dead-end, both in our own nation and in the League of Nations. It seems like the stormiest phase of the Karelian issue has already passed and everything is returning to its customary quiet state. But we know that the silence is the silence of a moribund people and the peace is illusory. The silence masks limitless suffering. And because of this, that silence is more horrifying than a clamor that can be heard up to the heavens.

Citizen! If you have even a smidgen of internal intuition that may allow you to see and hear what happens now beyond the border, you will see, across the hundreds of miles of wilderness, flames striking into the houses of our tribal brothers from Voznesenye to Kirov, and you will hear the groans of agony of the people of Kaleva.[37]

Have a look around yourself and see! There are thousands of exiles from the land of dying songs, so hear, *hear* the lamentation from their lips. At least here they are not forced to eat bark bread-like at home, but nevertheless, their hearts yearn day and night for the miserable land of Karelia, simply because that is their Fatherland. Hear them sing the same hymn as the Chosen People exiled in foreign lands:

---

[37] "People of Kaleva" (kalevan kansa) is a phrase that is difficult to translate. It is related to the title of the Kalevala, Finland's national epic, which means literally "land of heroes." In the context it is used here, it simply means the people of Karelia.

By the rivers of Babylon, there we sat down, yea, we wept, when
we remembered Zion. Now how shall we sing the Lord's song in
a strange land? If I forget thee, O Jerusalem, may my right hand
forget its skill.

It is with the greatest anguish that the citizen who loves his homeland asks: was it in vain that those generations of Finns and Karelians lived and died for their Fatherland over the centuries? Were they mere hallucinations that those visionaries experienced, when they saw the shattered Finnic tribe united one day, with borders that correspond to our tribal area? The Proto-Finnic people were shattered centuries ago, although at one time they spread from the Altay Mountains across all central and northern Russia, and the southern border of their territory stretched from the Bay of Riga to the south of where Moscow is now, to the great Samara bend.[38] Many of our lost and shattered brethren people already have vanished into the endless steppes of Russia, but remaining shards by the banks of the Volga, Oka, Kama, Ob, Pechora, Vychhegda, Irtysh, and Danube, in the areas of Kazan, Tver, Novgorod, and St. Petersburg tell of the monumental battles our people have had to endure during our millennia of wandering the desert. They have their own names, the Mordovian, the Vogul, the Vote, the Magyar; they all have their roots in the great Finnic tribe. Still, there have always been those who have had the strength to dream of a great united tribe and have not hesitated to sacrifice themselves for the sake of this dream. Now that it seems that the final fate of Karelia will be yet another in the series of tragedies for the Finnic peoples, one asks: were the dreams mirages? Where the sacrifices in vain? And yet these years are not far in the past, when it seemed like, to use Kalevalan allegory, the sun trapped within a mountain would for once shine upon us. Finland awoke, so did Estonia, and the shackles of centuries were finally broken. Ingria made the attempt, but the tribe of Kullervo

---

[38] Samara is the largest bend in the river Volga in Russia

fell on their own swords. The men of Karelia raised their swords, but the dawn of liberty in Karelia was extinguished in blood. The Magyars of Pusta were struck down in a great war in the land of Sándor Petőfi. Hungary was claimed by Romania, Yugoslavia, and Czecho-Slovakia, and now the undivided Tisza and Danube are under foreign rule. Thus Trianon became for Greater Hungary, what Tarto is for Finland and Karelia.

Those eternal seers, the mighty Kalevalan wizards who saw so much, did they see this? For all the suffering of Finnish warriors in the battles of yesteryear, must they now suffer this too? For the Finnish people, it is natural that there is distress in Karelia. It is something we are used to by now. It is almost considered a national trait of the Karelian people. This is why Finns no longer care about the messages arriving from there. It is heartbreaking to see the utter indifference displayed toward our younger siblings, and in fact also toward our own lifeblood issues. And precisely this depressed state of our national self-esteem and non-existent nationalist awareness is the basic, underlying cause for the present hopeless state of affairs. Accusations have been made toward consecutive governments, who during these years have handled the Karelian issue in an entirely unworthy manner, or else neglected it altogether. And these accusations are not baseless in the least.

But on the other hand, it should be noted that our people have never demanded more robust action from the government in this matter. It is useless to expect any kind of determined action from a government whose main effort is to first put itself together and then to resign later. Party politics have tied the hands of every government and prevented any kind of independent politics for the benefit of the entire nation. This is why the government vacillated between formal and unofficial neutrality during the Karelian wars, and the blood of lads was spilled in vain in the wilderness. The agreements in the Tarto peace treaty regarding Karelian or Ingrian autonomy have been left unenforced, which was the very reason for the Tarto agreement to begin with! In essence, we have permitted our eastern neighbor to defile the Finnish nation's honor right outside our border. And now, finally, we have removed the entire Karelian question from our foreign policy agenda, that is, if we can be said to even have one. Our government has washed their hands of Karelia and expect the issue to be dealt with in the League.

And what has the League done? In 1923 it was determined that the Karelian question was to be an international one. This indeed is an important acknowledgment as far as making the world aware of the issue and gaining sympathy for it. But it is still likely that the matter will drown in a sea of paper in the League. And the Finnish government will never have any greater clout in the League until we can present a "fait accompli," that is, tell them that this is what we have done, you have no option but to accept it. And for us to one day reach that point, we must find the solution in the Finnish people, and above all, in its youth. The lads who suffered cold, hunger, and homesickness in German trenches, watching for the Russians, dreaming of a free Fatherland, surely imagined it different than what it is now. Those lads surely did not imagine that the spring of liberty would be followed by a blackthorn winter of political squabbling and loss of unity that we now wallow in. Those youth who, even dressed in rags, were still Finns who struck terror in the Russians' hearts in battlefields in Estonia, Narva, the Paju Manor, the bloody squares of Marienburg and Pechory, at the gates of St. Petersburg, in three years of war in the wilderness of Eastern Karelia, along with our Karelian brothers. They never imagined our tribal bonds could one day shatter as they now have. At the time, they dreamed of something else and set different goals for themselves. Therefore, their hearts are being torn apart with anguish, which in this situation nevertheless is a boon in and of itself.

Simply because of this, the absolute necessity of our people waking, at last, it is the youth who must break the gridlock. Young men of this country must remind the people that at least among their own ranks the instincts that drove them to the battlefields of

Germany, Finland, Estonia, Ingria, and Karelia are still felt. It is a nationalist and patriotic awakening that this people need, and who else shall give it to them than those men whose comrades are now resting under rotting wooden crosses. Finland must either stand or fall with Karelia. The Finnish people must share either glory or degradation with the Karelians. This is why I say, that *Finland has not yet been*, just as there is no real Finnish people yet; there is still much work to be done for that to become a reality. We need love, a love that expresses itself in a passion for the Fatherland, for love with no passion is not love at all. We need labor, of the kind that asks no payment or glory, the kind carried out with mortarboard in one hand, a rifle in the other, from the morning call of life to its nighttime vigil, even if this ruins our sleep at night and daytime peace. We need loyalty, a truly Finnish loyalty, where each and every one of us stands on his own allotted spot in defense of the Fatherland, no matter how small or unimportant, because after all, our end goal is equally great for everyone. For this great work, we need all of our people. This is why we must wash the nightmare of "red" and "white" Finns from our eyes. There must be no lords and no workers in this country, no free men or slaves, only those who have a Fatherland and those who do not. And for this, we need also the Karelian people. Young refugees from Karelia! The song of liberty has not yet gone completely silent in Karelia. The *kantele* of Shemeikka and Onoila[39] have gone silent, but Kintismä and Usma continue to sing with the liberty of roaring rapids. Hear that call and join us; we Finnish men open our ranks for you. You shall become the 27th Jäger Battalion, whose wrath is invincible and who strikes deep;[40] you will clear a new path there where Karelia's misfortunes seem to have blocked it for good. For after all the great statesman's words are true: it is with fire and iron that the world is built. It is power that decides the fates of nations on the

---

[39] "Shemeikka and Onoila" two famous Karelian folk musicians.

[40] "Whose wrath is invincible and who strikes deep" is a reference to the "Jäger March," composed by Jean Sibelius, words by Heikki Nurmio who served in the 27th Jäger Battalion of the Imperial German Army.

great competing field. The Russian has never understood any other language than that spoken with bayonets. We know very well that minute by minute we go toward the great marathon, where both our and Karelia's fates will be decided. Therefore, we must prepare to face that moment eye to eye, for it is coming whether we want it or not. We must take into consideration the possibility that we will not be the equal of the mission and we shall receive defeat rather than victory. Should that happen, we must accept the defeat—may God forbid it—with the stoicism of Saarijärven Paavo: "the Lord may give and take away, but He will not forsake."

As long as we and the generations that come after us retain our faith in the God of our ancestors, our people will rise from the blood and ashes again to face this harsh land and the Russian yet again. For if God is with us, who can stand against us? *Finland has not yet been. Finland is yet to come.* We must be content to work toward this, even if our own eyes will never see the Greater Fatherland. Our hope remains that future generations one day will see it. But our goal must never be any less than leaving this country and its people to the future generations even greater than it is now. And then the land and people of Karelia shall be free. People of Finland: it is you who shall achieve this, and in doing so you must trust, next to God, in nothing but yourself. To prepare for that moment, content yourself with adding bark to your bread, for your neighbor's harvest is entirely gone. Raise your eyes to the hills. Collect your strength, unite your ranks, hear the call of your rising youth! It is the call of your own blood.

On the Feast of Memory

10th Anniversary Celebration of the Liberation of Oulu,
Organized by Volunteer Veterans, February 3, 1928

The hourglass of time indicates that it has now been 10 years since
the final shots rang out here, in the capital of Northern
Ostrobothnia, to signal that the rule of the Russians had been
broken. And then the trains began to roll toward the south, to
those locations where the claws of the enemy were still embedded
in the breast of our Fatherland. The memories of those days,
already somewhat faded by time, return vividly now, as I see
scarred faces, many of whom I recall standing side by side with
under the same flag. It is not possible to meet here without
becoming emotional. Even if we are separated from each other in
terms of location and geography, we have remained one during
these ten long years of separation. Of course, we have never been
as united as we were when we shared everything: victories,
defeats, hardship, and joy.

Many winters have passed since that one, each one after winter
1918 different than the one before. During bitingly cold weather I
am always reminded of the bitter cold we had to endure in the
snowbanks of Satakunta and Tavastia. A walk across a field in
moonlight reminds me of a night spent awake under a star-
studded sky when skiers clad in white cloaks would push through
the snow, rifles across their backs. Many a spring has also come
after the spring that followed that winter. But every year when
one feels for the first time the approaching spring in the air, one is
reminded of that particular spring, when, in the words of the poet,
"the great harvest of Finnish freedom" came to pass. Our troops
are now scattered all over Finland, but even those of us, who no

longer make their home here in Ostrobothnia, cannot forget the plains where we were born and raised. We cannot forget the people, whose love of freedom is also in our souls. And how could we forget the old Oulu standing in the middle of the plain, the eternal roar of the Merikoski rapids, the proud cathedral, and least of all, the graves of our heroic dead around it? All this we have in common, and it has kept us together all these years.

Above all, we have done so for the sake of all the hardship we have endured and for the sake of those who rest under the burial mounds, for, after all, a part of ourselves is there as well. How clearly do the memories of the battles of Oulu and the departure to the south return to us now!

Many of us were so young at the time that we did not fully understand the severity of our task. This became clear when during the train voyage some of us feared that the war would be over by the time of our arrival so that we might miss the excitement. It was apparent in the heedless bravery that made many lads climb above the stones to defy death and danger and also in the envy which caused some to lay claim to stolen valor. And these were troops that had not been trained for combat. They included schoolboys who had no experience of anything more severe than juvenile fistfights on the streets of Oulu. There were public servants, farmers, and workers who took their place in the battle, following only the instincts inherited in the blood of their ancestors.

As we were departing, our great mission was not yet clear to every one of us. But it certainly clarified itself to us when our hearts cried while listening to a dying comrade draw his final breath when we saw the endless distress of our Fatherland as it was torn apart, as we watched burning villages light up the night sky, as we charged toward the enemy with death racing at our heels. It was only then that the Fatherland revealed its true face to us. It was only then that the true, burning love for it was lit, as we rested on the cold land, in shared suffering with the torn Fatherland. We have men here from the three companies and artillery; we have infantry, grenadiers, and medics, whose memories will still vibrate when they hear such names as Vilppula, Vaskivesi, Kuru, Suodenniemi, Kyröskoski, Mouhijärvi, Tampere, Karkku, Vesilahti, Lempäälä, and Vyborg, among many others. We must never feel shame for the memories associated with those places, no matter what our ideals of honor may evolve into in this country. May these memories be passed on to the next generations, to continue to remind them of the most glorious days of our history, as they have been described by the poet: "Give thanks to the limitless courage, that lives in the icy North, give thanks to that precious blood that was spilled to secure the future."[41]

If such memories carry men to the pages of history, let the names written there be especially of our Jägers, those who charged into the fire with such joyful abandon. When the Jäger showed no fear, it meant that we also must not. When the Jäger refused to give up, neither did we. We still remember how it felt, when upon returning from a battle we received a casual compliment from a Jäger, or when fatigue, hunger, or cold threatened to defeat us, a Jäger's harsh encouragement poured new strength into our starving souls. Ostrobothnian skiers still remember that bloody night in Anttoora, when we saw the Jäger's green broadcloth coat under the white ski shirt, and our dying hope was revived and defeat seemed like victory. Those who marched from Mäntyharju toward the south remember: when dust coated our skin, our boots were filled with blood, and the weight of our packs on our numb shoulders seemed overwhelming, the sight of a Jäger's green coat in the front kept us marching.

But we must not be arrogant, as if this all was our own achievement. It was the God of our forefathers who carried and guided us in everything; it was Him we turned to when lying in the trenches in snowy forests; it was Him we addressed when we

---

[41] From "Tales of Ensign Stål" by Runeberg.

crossed our frostbitten fingers. It was a worthy battle we fought in the front. More worthy still was the battle of righteous mothers and fathers in each village in Ostrobothnia, when they prayed to the living God with anguished worry in their hearts. For it must be said, that all that is good that has happened to this country has been through mercy, for which we are merely the weak vessels.

The people of Finland cannot afford to be arrogant for another reason as well: because they left their freedom war unfinished. Our national spirit was waking, but it had not yet reached its full bloom. Therefore, we could have seen dizzying perspectives only a living sense of nationalism can allow a people to see. This is who did not see all of which we were capable. We did not reap the harvest of our freedom war; we were not yet prepared at the time. We did not strike the Russian as the song of men of the Cudgel War[42] declares, "He whom we strike down, is down for good."

For this reason, Greater Finland did not come to pass at the time, when the possibility was there, if only we had seized it. The troops who fertilized the Karelian soil with their blood in many years of war, striking terror into Russian hearts, did not receive reinforcements. They were driven apart. However, returning from there they brought with them a spark of the great ideal in their breast, and they swore that just as they believe in one almighty God, they believe in one, great Finland and its great future. "Tavastia, Karelia, the shores and lands of the White Sea, there is only one Great Finland!" Those are the words of the march we sang in the days of the Freedom War. Therefore, this day also cannot be just a day of memories, but also a day of great visions for the future. We must not forget the great ideal of our people: Greater Finland, not now, but in the years to come.

---

[42] The Cudgel War was a peasant rebellion in the Satakunta region of Finland in 1596-97.

With Clear Eyes

"As much as I believe in one almighty God, I believe in one Great Finland and its great future."

These words have been repeated year after year by the young men swearing their holy oath before their God, their Fatherland, and the flag of the AKS. They have been written indelibly in their souls. These same are now standing guard all over the Finnish peninsula carrying out their work, the work many believe to be modest. Nevertheless, they spend their time and energy carrying out the work required by their oath, making our flag's honor their own. This oath has been repeated, sometimes quietly within their souls, by generation after generation of men, who have made certain that neither the sword nor the spade have ever fallen from Finnish hands.

Our people have waded in deep waters throughout their history. Only fear of the Lord has carried them through thus far and kept us from drowning utterly. Our people have risen again and again from blood and ashes, but have never bent over, never been utterly crushed. We have had no inheritance to leave for their children apart from the ruins of their homes and the love and hate of generations. Our people have schooled themselves in log cabins with no chimneys. When the grain froze in the fields, they buried their teeth in the bark of a pine tree and stated, "The Lord gives and takes away, but never abandons us."

It was to the Lord young men turned, crossing their frostbitten fingers while lying in the snow that winter, where the great blood sacrifice, the freedom sowing of Finland was made. It was the strong hand of the Lord that led our people out of the slavery of

Egypt. Let the words of the Lord spoken to Israel be a warning to us as well, "Thou shalt have no other gods before Me."

I know here in this hall there are men who wish not to be reminded of sin, but as one who carries the coat of Lutheran priest, the words of the Lord are mine as well: "I have posted watchmen on your walls, Jerusalem; they will never be silent day or night."

Our people worship false gods, and in the absence of great contrition, this final fragment of the Finnish tribe here in the furthest north will drown in the swamp of sin and godlessness. Betrayal slithers on the people's breast, in the form of the serpent of communism.

The faith of our forefathers has been abandoned, love of the Fatherland is in ruins, respect for the authorities has gone, replaced by criminality. But even some of those people, whose heart is still moved by the fate of the Fatherland and the people, serve a foreign god. Some have made gold their false idol. Others bend the knee to the bottle, which contains a dragon's venom. For many, sacrificial smoke rises from the altars of obscenity all day and night. This is why the very ground shakes under our feet. This is why, in this era of frivolity, our dance may very well lead us to dance to our graves.

This causes the true patriot grief, and he cannot but spend day and night pleading to the Lord, that He may yet once again forgive our people. A real and living relationship with God creates a deeper love of the people than anything else since after all, its real focus is on the people's immortal souls. As an example, think of Moses, who led his people through the wilderness to the Promised Land. When Israel was met with divine wrath, Moses said, "But now, please forgive their sin—but if not, then blot me out of the book you have written." Such was the prophet, who wept for the downfall of his people on the smoking ruins of Jerusalem declaring, "Oh, that my head was a spring of water and my eyes a fountain of tears! I would weep day and night for the slain of my people. My heart is faint within me. Since my people are crushed, I am crushed; I mourn, and horror grips me." Such was Paul, who said: "For I could wish that I myself were cursed and cut off from Christ for the sake of my people, those of my own race," and yet, his only reward from his own people were chains and a back that had been flogged till it bled.

This is the spirit that is demanded of you, who now stand under this flag, demanded of you by God and the people. And above all, by the youth who still believe in the resurrection of Finland, Karelia, and Ingria. You must swiftly move to strike down the altars of false gods, whether they be in their own hearts, their homes, or in the Fatherland. Every inch of this country is too precious to ever be trodden by the enemy's feet. Our dream of a free Karelia and Ingria and a great Fatherland is too precious for it to perish in the embrace of sin.

I mentioned Karelia, the very name of which in the not distant past would create a wonderful spell through the minds of young men. Now when that name is spoken, it is as if the dark spirit of sorrow walks through our silent hall, with loud footsteps. The people are Karelia wander the Earth as refugees, singing the mournful song of the people of Israel in the past: "By the rivers of Babylon, there we sat down, yea, we wept, when we remembered Zion."

The Karelian cause is now said to be at a dead end. But I wish to remind you, that it never will be, not for as long as there are young men in Finland who still desire to sacrifice for the Fatherland, for Karelia, Ingria, for Greater Finland. Members of AKS! Let us be sure, that we can one day stand with clear eyes before the judgment of the coming generations.

The Lord's Vineyard in the North

Fundraiser at Kuopio Cathedral Held for the Benefit of Ingrian Christians, January 26, 1930

I will sing for the one I love a song about his vineyard: My loved one had a vineyard on a fertile hillside. He dug it up and cleared it of stones and planted it with the choicest vines. He built a watchtower in it and cut out a wine press as well. Then he looked for a crop of good grapes, but it yielded only bad fruit. "Now you dwellers in Jerusalem and people of Judah, judge between me and my vineyard. What more could have been done for my vineyard than I have done for it? When I looked for good grapes, why did it yield only bad? Now I will tell you what I am going to do to my vineyard: I will take away its hedge, and it will be destroyed; I will break down its wall, and it will be trampled. I will make it a wasteland, neither pruned nor cultivated, and briers and thorns will grow there. I will command the clouds not to rain on it." The vineyard of the Lord Almighty is the nation of Israel, and the people of Judah are the vines he delighted in. And he looked for justice, but saw bloodshed; for righteousness, but heard cries of distress.

(Isaiah 5:1-7)

The Lord planted a valuable sapling, in the form of the people of Israel. He surrounded it with a protective fence when He gave them His holy laws. He spoke sweetly of this garden he had made, "I will sing for the one I love a song about his vineyard: My loved one had a vineyard on a fertile hillside."

The word of God tells us how the Lord sent his servants, the prophets, to look for fruit in his vineyard. But they found nothing but the bloody fruit of sin. After this, he sent his own Son to find fruit, and they killed Him too. Then the garden met with the

Lord's punishment, and this prophecy came true: "I will make it a wasteland, neither pruned nor cultivated, and briers and horns will grow there. I will command the clouds not to rain on it."

Now God's chosen people wander the Earth shattered into pieces. There is an old wall near the temple courtyard in Jerusalem, the Wailing Wall, where the remains of Israel gather to lament their fate, to kiss the stones covered in moss and moan, "O God, why have you rejected us forever? Why does your anger smolder against the sheep of your pasture?"

Here in the north, the Lord has created a place for his vineyard. He has found it precious, given it elders and teachers, and through them allowed the land to flourish. Our people have waded in dangerous waters throughout their history, but the Lord has always guided us enough so that we have not altogether drowned. And when frost or the enemy's sword has struck the land and made it into a desert, the Lord has moved his hands to bring clouds over it and allowed the waters to revive the dead land. Our people have been schooled in log cabins with no chimneys, and when their grain has frozen in the fields, they have crossed their hands and said: "The Lord gives and takes away, but never abandons."

At the moment I would like to address the plantation that the Lord has created in the land of Ingria. On the banks of the river Narva, up to the gates of St. Petersburg, this Finnic tribe of a few hundred thousand have lived in modest huts covered in hay, maintaining their Finnish mind and following the pure teachings of Luther. Their story of survival among Slavic blood is heroic, if unwritten in the pages of history. With the Lord's strength, they have always risen again through the centuries, defeated, but never destroyed, leaving the love and hope of generations to their children.

Now, the unhappy nation of Ingria groans on its deathbed. They would like us to know how they cast their hopes on Finland when we too dreamed of a free Fatherland. But they no longer have the strength to speak; only a final groan issues forth from their throats, a final call for help to the cold, selfish Finland, whose own ranks are falling apart in internal strife. They would like to reach out from behind a barbed-wire fence, but they cannot — the hand is limp, growing cold as if in death. They wish to ask that those who still can, would shed tears for their children. They would gather in their temples, as their fathers and their fathers' fathers did, to pray that the dawn of resurrection may still rise over ruins and graveyards. But the doors of the churches are closed, and fathers, mothers, and God-fearing youth have had to pray on their knees outside their darkened churches. The Christmas star did not shine over Ingria this last Christmas, but rather the bloody star of Soviet Russia.

I have spent some time with them in Estonian Ingria, where the waves of the Great War swept a few fragments of the Ingrian people. I have seen them look with despair over the barbed wires, where the domes of their native church in Kosemkina shine over their homeland.[43]

They would like to build a church, but for them to be able to pick up the ax they need help from Finland. I have heard them sing in the Kalliviere chapel: "When will the morning star appear on my skies?"[44]

If only the Lord in all His mercy would allow that morning star to appear through the helping hand of friendship! What kind of fruit do the Finnish people harvest, here in the Lord's vineyard, so that we may be the only shard of the Finnic tribe left here in the North, to carry on the legacy of the splintered Finnic tribe?

It must be said that the grapes grown here are sour. Our people are about to drown in the swamp of their own sin and godlessness, yet they live without a care, even if they are standing above an open grave. Our intellectuals have blown the burning poison of atheism over the vineyard, causing the work of fathers and mothers to wither and die. Communism makes its way here,

---

[43] Those Ingrian churches that were not destroyed were sealed so that it was not possible to enter.

[44] Hymn by Anders Odhelius.

destroying altars to the Lord in the homes of workers. And in its footsteps comes another graven idol, "folk above all." In the midst of this devastation, a desensitized youth dance senseless, deaf to the agony of their homeland under their feet. Neither do they hear the lamentations from the other side of the border. Their ears have been deafened by the racket of dance drums. Had the Lord, that constant gardener, not saved even these fruitless trees, we would already have surely perished! Here, even in this church, there surely are those of whom the Lord has said: "Chop it off, since for some many years I have waited for fruit, but all it does is drain the land."

That father, that mother drain the soil in the Lord's vineyards, everything withers around. That one lad drains my circle of comrades, he must be cut away so that he does not drain those who seek new meaning in life. We have heard plenty of crashing lately, many young and old have been felled, as the blade has risen and fallen in the vineyard. Why have I been spared? Why have you? Only because the pierced hand of the heavenly gardener has stopped the blade, and He has prayed: "Let him be one more year, perhaps he will still bear fruit."

Our whole nation has been spared because of this same mercy; our only salvation has been because of intercession by Jesus. Imagine what a mercy it is for this nation, that the Lord has His followers among us, those who carry the sins of all, as their own. The Lord's cloud will rain upon this congregation as well; the father and mothers who weep for His harvest will see the rain fall through this scorching desert. They carry their children upon the arms of their prayers, asking Him to intercede on their behalf.

There are also those who now realize their formerly wasteful ways, feel sorrow by their own fruitlessness, and now irrigate the spent soil around them with their tears. To them, I say, with the words of the prophets (Isaiah 43: 18-19):

Forget the former things;
Do not dwell on the past.
See, I am doing a new thing!
Now it springs up; do you not perceive it?
I am making a way in the wilderness
And streams in the wasteland.

The Lord creates. His works are already apparent in the harvest of prayer by those who have awakened. It can be seen in the work of those who have sworn to devote themselves to the Fatherland, Karelia, and Ingria.

Yes, I mentioned Karelia, the very name which can create a mysterious stir in the men whom one day carried Karelia's pain in their hearts as their own, back to their own sleeping folk. Now the people of Karelia are, just like those of Ingria, with no mercy, with no Fatherland. Those who still live for the Lord will still pray on their behalf so that the Lord would break their yoke, the lash on their back, and the staff of their enslavers.

Our dream of a free Karelia and Ingria is too precious to be soiled by the embrace of sin. Let this truth be heavy on our conscience. Above anything else, our Fatherland needs true and faithful citizens whose hearts burn for our nation and people. And so do Karelia and Ingria, who languish in oppression and betrayal. If only the Lord, in His mercy, would awaken our people. Then He would see the miracle of which the prophet speaks (Isaiah 35:1-2):

The desert and the parched land will be glad;
The wilderness will rejoice and blossom.
Like the crocus, it will burst into bloom;
It will rejoice greatly and shout for joy.
The glory of Lebanon will be given to it,
The splendor of Carmel and Sharon;
They will see the glory of the Lord,
The splendor of our God.

A Christian Love for Tribal Brethren

Summer Meeting of Finland's Christian University
Students Association, Kuopio, August 10, 1930

A Christian's fatherland is above, and here on Earth, he is a guest and foreigner, with no permanent abode. Because of this, the Lord's Own search for their Fatherland as weary travelers and wait for their moment of eternity. But as they wait with longing in their hearts in this ditch of mercy, it is nevertheless in the priceless Fatherland that their own fathers have spent their Earthly travels in. They know that they come from this land and that they will again become of this land.

Because of this, each palm's width of this land is too precious to be trodden upon by the enemy's feet. Above all, this land is precious for them, because it is lived in by a people who are flesh of their flesh and blood of their blood. A true and living love toward God has always created a deeper and more true love toward one's own people than anything else, for it is concerned with the immortal souls of the same people, whose blood they can hear pumping in their own veins.

Such a devoted love toward his own people was that of Moses, who led the people of Israel through the wilderness to the Promised Land. When God's ire was raised toward the people worshiping idols, he wished the Lord to erase him from his books, if He could not forgive his people. Such were the prophets, who wept at the diminishing and suffering of their peoples. And such was the Apostle of the Lord Paul, who said to his next of kin: "Who is weak, and I do not feel weak? Who is led into sin, and I do not inwardly burn?" Dear audience members! I have been asked to give a speech in this student celebration on the topic of love toward our tribal brothers. If the woeful fate of our tribal brethren would weigh on our conscience, we could no longer be merry. If the Lord were to hold us accountable for our own sins, we could no longer look without sympathy to him who carries a burden that is larger than he can bear.

I do not now wish to speak of the Forest Finns cut down in the woods of Värmland[45] – they are no longer there. I do not speak of the spiritual darkness in which that the Finns of Finnmark[46] and Länsi-Pohja[47] currently dwell, even though the Komi who dwell by the rivers Vychegda and Vym lead a much better life than them. I do not speak of those remnants of our tribal brethren, whose swansong is heard along the Volga and both sides of the Urals. They are dragging themselves to their graves, and our love can no longer reach them.

I *do* ask this group of students, gathered here in your white caps, to take a moment in the midst of this celebration to listen to the groans of moribund Karelia and Ingria. The Karelian people, who have walked their Via Dolorosa for a millennium, now lie bloodied and dying. For their wounds, they can barely raise their head any longer, but with their last effort, they look to Finland, hoping for rescue at the last moment. Do we have a Christian love toward our tribal kin? Love for the refugee, who while eking out a modest living here still dare to maintain embers of hope in their heart? Is there anyone here, whose soul has not been burned by the spiritual strife of these refugees, those for whom there is no homeland or mercy? Each time I have the opportunity to discuss tribal issues, it seems like I must act as an interpreter for those mute warriors, whose mouths are filled with earth from Neva and Svir all the way to where the shore is beaten by the waves of the Arctic Ocean. It has been said that their blood was spilled in vain, but blood can never be spilled in vain. That blood calls from the

---

[45] Värmland is a region is western Sweden, where the so-called Forest Finns settled during the 16th Century. They are now assimilated into mainstream Swedish society and their culture and language are extinct.
[46] Finnmark (Finnish: Ruija) is a region in Norwegian Lapland.
[47] Länsi-Pohja: (Swedish Vasterbötten) is a region in northeast Sweden that borders Finland.

earth to the Seat of Grace for forgiveness for the land for which it has sacrificed itself. If only that cry would wake up the conscience of the people, who had the luxury of sitting mute in their homes, not hearing the cries rising from the lips of our poor tribal brothers in the dark years of the Karelian freedom struggle. Did those men who fought side by side with the Karelian and Ingrian peoples have Christian love in their hearts? Only God knows. We do not; we can only guess. We have seen many of them cross their frostbitten hands in prayer over a rifle in the woods of Karelia and seen them fall in the snow with a final prayer on their lips. In any case, their example has helped awaken sleepy Christians to this request, as the hymn says: "I may have the name of a Christian; now make me into a true Christian!" And those who have shared the ecstasy of victory and the misery of defeat with them cannot but bless them. Our love has been called a hopeless and unhappy love. But why should we forget Karelia? Why should we forget those who fought with them? Why should we not remember this youth, whom we carried through the wilderness toward the Gulf of Finland, with their blood spilling between ours? How could we forget those comrades, whose final sighs pierced our hearts, but whose lips never spoke a single curse against the lack of manliness of the Finnish people? One of our final sights before leaving Karelia was a young Ostrobothnian lad, lying dead and bloody, hanging from barbed wires, with the bayonet of his rifle still pointing toward the enemy's trenches. The bayonet that fell from the hand of a 13-year-old lad is still waiting to be picked up by a hand driven by a newly awakened Christian love. The people of Ingria, who number a few hundred thousand, are fighting for their existence on the banks of the Narva to the gates of St. Petersburg, it seems for the last time ever, in their millennium of struggle. They are mired in slavery and horror and can no longer remember how many times they have dreamed of freedom and been disappointed.

Their mute, silent distress is greater than any words can express. Some time ago a certain Ingrian poet, who had been living in Helsinki as a refugee, left for a final voyage onto the ice covering the Gulf of Finland and never returned. Before his departure he wrote, "I believe that dawn will yet come for the people of Ingria, and I should remain strong until then. I should have the strength to pray for it to come soon, the strength to believe that it will yet come."

The poet could no longer wait for the dawn; his heart was overwhelmed, as Bobi Sivén's heart in Repola. They are still waiting for their daybreak, the people whom I have heard sing in Estonian Ingria, looking longingly past the barbwire fences, "When will the morning star appear on my skies?" Please hear me: a Christian's love will yet light a morning star in the sky over suffering Ingria. But for this to happen, our responsibility is tremendous. God in his mercy has awakened the tiny herd of Finland and given them a will to victory. God's people need yet another awakening so they can act as His instrument in bringing about the time when they may serve their Lord in a Greater Fatherland. We do not yet see this time other than in our imagination, as if through a mist of tears. Yet we raise our eyes to the heavens, and we know the light still shines there, even if we do not yet see it. We require a living Christian love, not one that spares flesh and blood, not one that is tender, but one that can serve as a weapon for a wrathful God, should He need one. Let Him awaken in us too, who in principle are awakened to the tribal question, a Christian love. For even if we were to sacrifice our bodies for our tribe, without love this would not benefit us or our beloved tribe in any way.

Toward the Storm

AKS Independence Day Celebration, December 6, 1931

While a group of youth dressed in the colors of the AKS celebrate the highest achievement of the Finnish people, it simultaneously remembers our tribal brethren peoples, for whom independence remains a dream. It is the fulfillment of this dream that they still continue to believe in, just as those who worked toward the dawn of Finnish independence once believed.

Ten years ago, some young Finnish lads celebrated their Independence Day far away in the Karelian wilderness, where they had rushed to, following the demands of their very blood. At this difficult time, when our nation is shaken by political fanaticism and upheaval, few can spare a thought for the plight of Karelia and Ingria. But at the very least those whose souls have been permanently marked by memories of our fellow peoples' war years, will still remember. The final, desperate struggle of Karelia began with the battles on the shores of the river Olonka and throughout the White Sea region. From the wilderness the men of Karelia came, driven by a desperate fury back to the ruins of their own villages, rushing to attack an enemy that outnumbered them many times over. Those, who have seen those ragged bands of forest guerrillas, with faces lined with suffering, skiing with arms powered by nothing but hatred toward fire and death, can only remember the words of the poet: "The heroes thus walk to their death."[48]

Even in defeat, the final freedom struggle of Karelia was a stout

---

[48] From the march "Vilppulan urhojen muistolle" ("to the Memory of the Braves of Vilppula") by Heikki Klemetti, 1918

promise of a national awakening in Karelia. The spark that brought about the battle was the desire for freedom of Karelian men, even if the blood they spilled mixed with Finnish blood. In the previous uprising in Olonets, it was almost exclusively Finnish volunteer forces who fought. They had, three years earlier, made their initial forceful push to the shores of the Svir and the outskirts of Petrozavodsk, but then were forced to retreat before an overwhelming enemy, and finally were shattered in the shrapnel fire of Vitelen and Tuulosjoki. The men of the northern front were undefeated, but nevertheless, they were left unaided and had to retreat to their homeland from the victorious battlegrounds of Matrosy, Polovina, and Suollusmäki.[49]

We know how the last Karelian uprising ended. Hunger, cold, and depleted ammunition exhausted those small bands of guerrillas in the frozen woods. Even in death, they colored the Karelian snowbanks with their enemies' blood, as well as their own. The last remnants of the regiments of wilderness guerrillas retreated to Finland, with the remaining hope that the signal fires will be one day ignited again over the Karelian hills. What the men of Karelia went through in those days, God only knows, the God that the guerrillas prayed to in the thick of battle: "Guard the warriors of Karelia who love Christ!" What suffering was the lot of the Karelian women, whose fate was described by the guerrilla's commander: "Everything that is painful and hopeless has been the fate of the women of Karelia. Sorrow is their only faithful companion; lamentation their song."

Intertwined with the Karelian question is the lack of nationalist spirit in Finland, to use the term coined by J. V. Snellman. This people's mentality, as a whole, has never displayed the fortitude necessary to carry out the Karelian cause to its proper ending, and it never will, for as long as they walk under the yoke of a foreign mentality. The Karelian freedom movement belongs, first and foremost, to the Karelians themselves, but the Finnish

---

[49] Suollusmäki (Russian Sulazhgora) is a neighborhood in Petrozavodsk

government must support it and enforce the rights of the Karelians. But they lack the moral support to do that, for even some Finnish citizens follow the bloody red star of Soviet Russia, and our leading intellectuals cozy up to Scandinavian culture, caring nothing for the fact that the birthing lands of their own culture are drowning in blood and tears. Because of this, the Finnish state has had to remove the Karelian question from its practical policies and has been unable to prevent the outrages to the Tarto agreement carried by Russia. We also understand that the Karelian question has been left to languish in the League of Nations, for lack of any convincing force to back up any demands. Because of this, the Karelian question is at a dead end, when it comes to official state policy. This is not the case for the Soviet Union, for their policy is the utter destruction of Karelia. These days, the Ingrian issue is even more urgent than that of Karelia. The cries of agony of the Ingrian people have only intensified since the Tarto agreement. Even the Finnish people awoke from their torpor for a moment last winter and early spring, when trains carrying exhausted remnants of the Ingrian people began to roll out of Ingria, toward death and oblivion in the mines of Murmansk and the gulags of Archangel and Siberia. Wailing was heard those spring nights from many Ingrian villages, and many women in Ingria have actually been driven mad by grief.

The Ingrian people are now without mercy, without a homeland. They wish to extend their hand toward Finland, asking for assistance from their sibling tribe, says a certain Ingrian poet, but it has not the strength, the hand is limp, it is as cold as death. They ask that those who still can would weep for Ingria, for they themselves have no more tears. An Ingrian mother writes from a gulag in Siberia:

The children are dying in droves here. They simply fall asleep and never awaken. Some die with their hand on their cheeks, some with their arms limply on their side. They are small martyrs, who die in innocence before beasts. My daughter passed away, with her

hand on her cheek. Hers is a martyr's crown, one no one can ever
deprive her of. Even if we never leave this place, we shall meet
again in the heavenly home. No one can take that away from us.

Some of these refugees have found safety within the Estonian and
Finnish borders. We have seen them in the Estonian part of Ingria,
living in tiny huts by the barbed wires on the border. There are
mothers, whose sons are imprisoned behind the walls of Kresty
or Solovki.[50] There are men whose comrades sleep underground
in the lands of Ingria, due to wounds sustained in Kaporye,
Oranienbaum, or Gatchina.[51] The noblest of them all was Leander
Reijo,[52] who in life was referred to as the king of Ingria. It is
because of his death that the AKS flag is now at half-mast. The
mournful message arrived from across the Gulf of Finland, that
he had fallen victim to an assassin, near the border he had always
hated with his heart. His noble heart beats no more, but the flame
of his spirit lives in the hearts of Ingrians who were inspired by
his words or by his heroic deeds. The Ingrian, who fell on his
lonely guard spot, is an example even to AKS members, especially
at a time when our determination seems to falter, and many are
in danger of forgetting the oath they swore that they would live
and die by.

The Finnish people are used to news of turmoil in Ingria. Once
the deportations began, Finland's government sent diplomatic
notes to Russia, and they in fact did stop for a while. But once our
attention wandered elsewhere, they began anew and continue to
this day. The Ingrian question has not been brought up in the
League of Nations. Our university students are continuously
scolded against taking too passionately a stance on this. There is
no need to warn the Finnish people of being too patriotic, this
most indifferent of peoples to the fate of their own tribal brethren.

---

[50] Kresty is a prison in the St. Petersburg area. Solovki prison camp was on one of the
Solovetsky Islands on the White Sea.
[51] Kaporye, Oranienbaum and Gatchina are locations in Ingria, now part of Russia.
[52] Leander Reijo (1904–1932) was an Ingrian tribal activist. He was kidnapped and taken to the
Soviet Union in 1931 and executed after a show trial.

Has it even displayed any sympathy toward them? It certainly managed to display remarkable indignation toward those who forced a few communists to leave the country the summer before last, more so than they ever did toward the rapists of the Ingrian lands. And at the time when messages of sheer horror arrive from Ingria, the Finnish parliament decides to deny assistance to soldiers injured in the Estonian Freedom War. And also to the disabled veterans of the Ingrian volunteer forces, because, it is true, there are a few cripples on this side of the Gulf of Finland, with legs or arms blown off when the Ingrian volunteers rushed toward Krasnaya Gorka.

But one day our people will awaken. This is a topic that has been repeated annually in the speeches, given under the AKS flag. And they must continue to be repeated until this actually happens. So many prayers have been said for this people, so many tears and so much blood has been shed, such a heavy burden has been set above their shoulders, that the times of national awakening are destined to come. "The pro-Finnish movement you elders refuse to understand," as J. V. Snellman says, "will one day triumph." And furthermore, "Once the people awaken, their awareness will be strong, so strong that nothing can oppose it."

The will for freedom lives on in our tribal kin peoples. It hides in the Karelian and Ingrian wilderness, defying all oppression. It lives in the hearts of refugees, whose homesickness burns in their hearts. It lives in the hearts of volunteers who shared their sufferings with the Karelians. How could they forget the comrades they carried toward the Finnish border, with blood tricking between their fingers!

The bodies of these lads are a letter addressed to the sleeping people of Finland, which reads: love has faith above all, hope above all, can withstand all. The work of Finnish volunteers was not in vain; they were, as it has been said, "pioneers of a great ideal, the ideal of unity for the Finnic race."

AKS has sworn to dedicate their work and their life to Karelia, Ingria, and Greater Finland. The future will tell if we can fulfill the hopes many attach to us. For it to happen, the men of AKS must first fight the battle in our hearts, even here in the midst of the entertainment and sophistication of our country's capital. The Karelian and Ingrian cause is too holy for it to be successfully advanced by men who have failed in their struggle against impropriety. The voice of AKS must continue to shout at the people, still mentally divided by political divisions, so that when the time is right, we can all act as one to bring about the freedom of Ingria and Karelia. Even if we never see this moment, we must work toward it so that future generations one day will see it. "That the work may progress slowly," as J. V. Snellman remarks, "is often humanly frustrating." But he continues, "Most must toil for the moment they themselves will never see, calmly passing on the work when their own journey is at an end."

Again we hear the storm gathering in the East. The Finnish people, divided by our own disagreements and in a time of great financial difficulty, will face this storm, whether we wish to or not. Voroshilov gathers his troops, troops whose hoof prints never grow grass, and the land of red twilight prepares once again to attack the peace-loving people of Finland, and after us, all of Western Civilization. But if we were to only awaken to the fear of God and a living sense of nationalism, we could face this storm with confidence.

Then, the Finnish people and tribe will find their place in the sun. The peoples of Karelia and Ingria will return to their abandoned lands. That was the dream of those guerrilla warriors during the Great Hatred, who once had to watch with impotent hate as the walls of St. Petersburg rose along the banks of the Neva River. Then the dream of lads lying in their graves in Karelia and Ingria will become a reality, a reality they never live to see. Then we shall see that the prayer of the Ingrian mother, who still tries to feed her child with the milk of her withering body beyond the mountains of Krasnoyarsk, has been answered. The dawn of resurrection will arrive above the graveyards and ruins of Karelia and Ingria. We must take courage and strength to wait till then, as the Ingrian poet Antti Tiittanen, whose heart burst in waiting: "We must have the strength to believe the day will come soon, strength to pray, that it may come at all."

We Must Not Forget

15th Anniversary Celebration of Oulu's Liberation During
The Finnish Civil War, Organized by Oulu White Guard
And Oulu Veterans' Association, February 3, 1933.

In these days of celebration, when we remember the glorious days of our own freedom war, the People of Finland must remember our kindred peoples, whose wars of liberation were so closely aligned to ours, but were damped out in fire and blood. As Finland's freedom dawned, the cries of Karelia and Ingria grew louder and louder. And this is why many Finnish men followed the call of our blood. Battalions of Finnish youth arrived at the banks of the river Svir the spring following the year of our freedom war. Elsewhere, they progressed toward Petrozavodsk, toward the domes of churches already visible to them. But under pressure from the battalions of Russians, they were forced to retreat from the victorious battlefields of Matrosy, Polovina, and Suollusmäki, or they were broken under shrapnel fire in Vitele and Tuuloksenjoki.

Yet again the signal fires were lit in the Karelian wilderness. Once again Northmen embarked on a revenge march across the border. However, the tiny guerrilla groups were exhausted by hunger, cold, and lack of ammunition, and they had to return with suffering carved on their faces, in tatters. Even in ruins, the freedom struggle of Karelia is a promise of national awakening, and Finnish youth saved Finland's military honor for the coming days. They were the pioneers of a great ideal, the ideal of a Greater Finland, at a time when our own government had our flag lowered down in Repola and Porajärvi,[53] as the articles of the shameful Tarto peace treaty demanded. Now the cries of agony can be heard from our east and southeast from behind barbed-wire fences, and these selfish people, so prone to turning on their own, will have to bow their heads in shame before the judgment of history, for not having the courage to make the heritage of the freedom war their own. The ill-disposed attitude of the people and the government of Finland was the first bitter disappointment for the frontmen of the freedom war. But soon after the entire patriotic segment of our populace had to bear the shame of a failed raid that ended in disappointment, and red laughter echoes in their ears both within and without our own borders. Our people forgot the red peril and allowed the red viper to lounge on its own breast.

But suddenly the miracle of the freedom spring repeated itself. The red wave was stopped. The men of Southern Ostrobothnia, whose blood is hotter than anyone else's in Finland, shouted from the plains of Lapua in each orientation: "No mockery of God nor Fatherland will be allowed on our plains." That shout was heard all over Finland, and in every municipality, we began to wash off the shame from the face of the Fatherland. If communism had been allowed to thrive in our country under the wings of liberal parliamentarism, the wish of a certain communist member of parliament could have become a reality: the Finnish coat of arms would have been replaced with the hammer and the sickle.

By crushing communism to the ground, the people of Finland managed to show that they still have the ability to carry out their historical mission, as the last line of defense of the West against the hellish East, for the time being at least. And for us veterans of the front lines, it was again slightly easier to visit the graves of our fallen comrades.

The citizen who loves his Fatherland looks to the future with anxiety. Again our future is covered with dark clouds. The

---

[53] Repola and Porajärvi are two central Karelian regions.

Eastern storm howls in our ears now and our people walk toward it, whether we wish it or not. Voroshilov gathers his troops, and the land of red twilight prepares to rush the gates of the West. From within, our country is shaken by economic hardship and shocks caused by political fanatics. And the blackest of our cardinal sins, which our people have carried since our dawn, before the dawn of civilization, mutual envy and distrust, threaten to again divide our people, at the time when we should be preparing to strike toward the East. This must not happen! The Finnish people must not forget our tremendous responsibility to the future.

For some among our people, the guiding star is the bloody star of Soviet Russia, and no manner of compromise or mediation is possible with them. Above all, the frontmen must stand on the same side of the barricade in times of war and peace. In the present spiritual battle, they must remember the words Napoleon spoke to his old guard: "The guard falls, but will not surrender." The front veterans form such an old guard, who have the old traditions to uphold. It cannot stand on no-man's-land; it cannot relent; it cannot withdraw. They must be a voice reminding our people that they must be united at the decisive moment. They must remind the new generations who dream of heroism that as grand as it is to die for the Fatherland, it is just as great to live for it, live a pure, unselfish life.

Our youth must be trained in a living, nationalist mindset and be given leaders with great vision, capable of molding history and under whose banners they can gather. There are always those wise and cautious who caution against excessive passion, as our minister of the exterior did when our youth was in uproar during the Ingrian crisis. The Finnish people can be accused of almost anything, but never of excessive patriotism — this has been shown by history a thousand times. Did not the years of our tribal freedom wars show that no people are as indifferent to the fates of the fellow members of their tribe? Do not our leading intellectuals fawn toward the Scandinavian civilization, when death and frost walk the birthing-land of our culture and life there drowns in tears and blood? The path of anyone who loves his Fatherland has always been harsh in this country — the harshest when we were languishing under foreign rule. The activists of those times had to deal with much misunderstanding and shame, directed at them by those who could not or dared not understand the clear vistas they saw in their souls. The patriotism of those times had to be free of any personal interest. They were rewarded with disgrace and exile rather than honor, imprisonment rather than freedom. Our generation has much to learn from their type of patriotism since it has the same nobility, self-denial, and sacrifice of all torch-bearers. On the other hand, that type of patriotism despises the mass-mentality of those who wish to remain impartial and observe the battle from afar, making sure that their own interests will be taken care of in the aftermath.

But above all, our people need a religious awakening. The cause of the Fatherland is so high and sacred, that it cannot be successfully advanced by those whose will has been broken by their own moral downfall. Our dream of a Greater Finland must not perish in the embrace of sin. The individuals who fight for it need pure ideals and a moral backbone. He whose ears are deafened by the rattle of jazz drums cannot hear the lamentation of Karelia and Ingria. Woe betide the youth of Finland, squandering their most valuable years in the frenzy of frivolous entertainment when the very land of their birth shakes beneath their feet! We need youth who fear God, and if we have them, we need nothing else.

Despite everything, we can see some signs of religious or nationalist awakening among our young people, and it is these people that the future belongs to. It is with the optimism of youth that we believe that we shall not drown in the storms we are now rapidly approaching. This country shall not be trampled by the hooves of the invading forces, as the Russians are predicting. The dawn of resurrection will one day reach across the graveyards and ruins of Karelia and Ingria, and the borders of Finland will reach as far as our might allows. If this generation will live to see it, God only knows. But for this to be possible we must maintain our old military traditions here too, in the plains of Northern Ostrobothnia. Fathers and Mothers must leave the same love and hate that has been our heritage from one generation to another.

The Crown of Thorns of Karelia and Ingria

AKS Gathering, February 22, 1933

Today, as I paid a visit to the AKS offices, I noticed a crown of thorns[54] placed on a map of Ingria.

That crown of thorns is made of the same iron that separates Finland and Russia and now squeezes Karelians and Ingrians to the Soviet Union so tightly that blood seeps from the folk body of our kindred peoples. As I stood gazing at the crown, I wondered, how much longer will the Lord allow the Ingrian people to carry it. They have carried it throughout their history, but now it has been pushed down on their heads tighter than ever since they have been bound by the articles of the Tarto peace treaty.

Eleven years have passed since the day that three men gathered here for the Karelian student association. They had returned from battles in the snowy woods of Karelia, seen our tribal brothers' uprising and brief dream of liberty until it was extinguished by Soviet machine gun fire. They had hoped to place a victor's laurel wreath on Karelia but instead saw it crowned with barbed wire. Because of this, the distress of Karelia and Ingria tormented them even here in the midst of a gay and sophisticated Helsinki, and therefore they took it upon themselves to create the AKS. They did not dare to think much would become of it, but now eleven years later, we see that growing numbers of youth come to us to swear, under our black flag, to spend their life for the Karelian and Ingrian cause and to never fail in their belief for Finland's future greatness. This is why

---

[54] The object mentioned here was made of the same barbed wire that was bloodied by the body of the "King of Ingria", AKS member farmer Leander Reijo, as he was ambushed and dragged across it from Ingria and Soviet Russia

this association is the greatest promise for the future, and one day we will pay the debt that Finland owes to our brethren people currently writhing in agony.

With astonishing tenacity, the AKS has survived the political storms that have shaken our people since the freedom war. The days of fiery excitement were followed by a strong reaction. Our people had to contend with the shame of a heavy retreat, leaving the AKS nearly alone in carrying on with the defensive battle against the mocking enemy who followed on our heels. Finally, a miracle happened. This time, we did not stop at the Siikajoki river, but rather after an uprising from the plains of Lapua, and communism was systemically struck down. The rise of the Patriotic People's Movement (Isänmaallinen kansallis-liitto, IKL) continues among our folk. The furious reaction against it proves that something important is taking place. The very fact that this movement has been resisted with a maniacal zeal proves its importance and vitality. The events that surrounded the creation of the AKS have been repeated with the People's Movement, and if its influence grows among the regular folk similarly as that of the AKS has among students, the future unquestionably will be theirs. Our association has already for more than a decade waited in vain for a political party to support us in our struggle for Karelia and Ingria.

Now, the IKL, with its signature courage, has included the idea of Greater Finland as the first item in their party agenda. The desire for liberty and greatness blows toward Finland's youth from the Ostrobothnian plains. The men of IKL are driven by the same unselfishness and willingness to sacrifice as the men in the front lines in the wars of Finland, Karelia, and Ingria, and therefore they also carry the promise of the Greater Finnish renaissance of the future. AKS must join the IKL in their struggle, however without losing their identity as a free academic association. We must maintain it both in times of peace and war.

The signs are clear: a great battle between two fronts in our society has begun. On one of these fronts, we have the forces who seek to preserve it; on the other, those who would destroy it. Once these fronts meet, there will be no "no-man's-ground" between them. The statues of the heroic fallen everywhere in our country constantly remind us of that. The tears of the comrades and families have never been properly dried; they shall remind us of our duty to their memory for as long as we live. We have no doubt at all that if the miracle of Verdun were to repeat itself, they would stand with us on the same side of the barricade.

It is no wonder that we advance our ideals in uncompromising and harsh ways. Our type of diplomacy was created in the front lines. The men of the AKS must never forget that the inheritance of the men who fought in the Karelian and Ingrian wilderness is theirs alone to carry to the future, and they must always honor the grim traditions that were created there. To the university students who take their place under our black flag, remember throughout your carefree student life, that Karelia and Ingria weep at the ruins of their villages, expecting more of us than some of us may realize. These expectations are shared by us since we remember those who once fought, but who are now hidden under Tuoni's cloak.[55] We hope for others to pick up their work from where they left. And if it is not the youth of the AKS who are to continue it, then no one will. The citizen who loves his tribe waits impatiently for the opportune moment, while the news from across the border grows more dismaying by the day. The AKS has the advantage of eternal youth, as new generations join its ranks. With the optimism of youth, the AKS believes that world history will soon enough create the right moment to join Karelia and Ingria to a greater Fatherland. Right at this moment, we are hearing the calls that will eventually lead to Karelian and Ingrian freedom all the way from Jehol and Manchuria. And we believe that the time will soon come when the Lord, using the arms of our youth, will lift off the iron crown of thorns from the bleeding foreheads of Karelia and Ingria.

---

[55] Tuoni is the god of the Underworld in Finnish folk religion.

The Dawn of Finland's Greatness

AKS Rally, May 29, 1933

In considering the present-day student politics, which affect the entire nation, it is wise to remember the words of J. V. Snellman when describing the student politics of his own day:

> I know rather well, that there are two trends present in our youth today: one of them is a positive, life-affirming trend that seeks to create something new. The other is only negative, defensive. This type of negativity is an unhappy trend for the nation and will end in its ruin. Only strong and manly action that aims to create anew will save the people and push them forward.

Dear citizens! I dare suggest that this positive and forward-looking type of belief has been represented by the Academic Karelia Society ever since its black flag was first seen in the students' flag parade. I will go on to say that one wonders what would have become of our student youth, without the ideals of the AKS to guide them forward. In the years following our wars of liberation, that spiritual tiredness and lack of vision that all of our people were falling into, seemed to plague student life as well.

Our people were led by those who were absent when the fate of the people was decided on a coin toss, with life or death as collateral. Unless perhaps these individuals had been present, but on the opposite side of the barricades. When the heroes of the freedom war were still licking their wounds, our people embarked on their retreat, with Russian mocking laughter at their back. The spiritual torpor students had sunk into barely allowed them to take notice of what type of peace treaty was made in

Tarto. They did not hear how the artillery of Fort Ino[56] went silent for good. They did not see how the Gulf of Finland became an inland sea for the Russians. Bobi Sivén's pistol shot was heard from Repola when the Finnish flag was taken down there for the last time. The Ingrian flag came down in Kirjasalo, as youngsters came back from Karelia. They told us that Karelian villages are burning from the shores of the White Sea to Lake Onega, of bloody battles in the distant Karelian wilderness, and of how Finno-Ugric cultures are now drowning in tears and blood.

This caused the new fires of national awakening to be lit among the students, the realization that they had yet to claim the inheritance of the freedom war that was theirs, and that their work would be incomplete for as long as Karelia and Ingria weep under a slave's yoke. During the battles of 1919, it was clear that Finnish national identity was not yet fully formed. The young men, who, starving and wearing rags, continued to make their way toward Onega and the river Svir, understood their task with the intuition of their youth, while those directing the student politics of the time did not.

As AKS began its own struggle, our perception of the lack of nationalist understanding among our people grew stronger still. Intellectuals of older generations, with a few exceptions, displayed nothing but indifference and arrogance toward the nationalist fervor arising in the students. They were unable to appoint leaders for this youth from among their number, leaders for which we have been hoping for 15 years.

Meanwhile, in Sweden, officers and public servants who had participated in our freedom were dismissed from their positions. Our own intellectuals were planning a celebratory Norden dinner with the Swedes. To those who would be our leaders and teachers, their priority seemed to be to express gratitude to Sweden as the transit nation of culture. However, in war, we had seen that we needed arms and ammunition more than culture, but as these

---

[56] Fort Ino was a coastal fortress on the Neva Bay.

were not delivered to us via Sweden, we remembered Snellman's words: "for such a people as the Finns, it is poor, if not utterly degrading, to consider themselves indebted to the Swedes."

The new Finnish nationalist ideal, Greater Finland, is not a product of some Hegelian philosophy. It was born on the battlefields of the freedom war and Eastern Karelia. But it also has gone through its own evolution as the main point of student politics. It became obvious that we must begin our struggle for the nationalist awakening of Finland as soon as possible so that the entire people would come to understand Snellman's immortal beliefs, which according to him, did include the idea of a greater homeland. If a people lack an expansionist striving for greatness, its nationalist feelings remain dormant. A people who have fallen into passivity are doomed to vanish from the pages of history. According to Snellman — and he stressed this point many times — the borders of nations must follow tribal borders. Snellman goes so far as to criticize the Maamme anthem,[57] by Runeberg, because it lacks a striving for greatness, which is present for example in the British national anthem "Rule, Britannia! Britannia, rule the waves! Britons never, never, never shall be slaves."

Not many words are required to describe our nationalist activities. There are none — at least as of yet. This is shown by the calm indifference that we observe the tragedy to the east and southeast of our border. If ever did the crown of thorns press against the foreheads of our tribal brethren peoples, then it is now. Unless rescue arrives by next fall, tens of thousands of Ingrians and Karelians will again be deported to the mines of Murmansk and Siberia, where there are already thousands of them, their bones in the dust.

There are ladies present in this gathering. Have you stopped to consider the fate of the women of Karelia and Ingria? It has been said, that the only companion whose company they can count on is grief, and lamentation the best portrayal of their inner

---

[57] *Maamme* ("Our Land") by Runeberg is Finland's national anthem.

life. A certain Ingrian, whose writing describes the fates of those deported to Siberia, also notes that many an Ingrian woman has lost her sanity. It is no wonder that the mind of anyone who cares for the fates of our brethren becomes clouded by depression when he notes how deeply the great Eastern raptor has sunk its claws into the hearts of our tribal brothers. Soviet Russia has developed into such a militaristic superpower, that for the first time in its own history it can stand fully on its own. Improved traffic infrastructures in Soviet Karelia have created optimal operational conditions for a full-fledged military invasion of Finland.

But even so, the great Eastern giant struggles not to come apart at the seams. Many of its minority peoples are rattling their own chains. Georgia, Turkestan, and the Caucasus are once again in turmoil. In Azerbaijan, there are more than ten different guerrilla groups now operating. Kazakhs, Tatars, and Finnic tribes from the Urals to our border and that of Estonia are waiting for the opportune moment to yank themselves free of the Russian national body. The geopolitical storm gathering in the East may suddenly develop into a real moment for Finland to act decisively on Karelia's behalf once and for all. The near future will show how the people of Finland brave the coming storm.

New signs of national awakening are emerging among our people. The AKS no longer fights alone; IKL rushes forward to carry the promise to the future. If this movement will reach the soul of the Finnish people, much depends on that. IKL is the first political party with the daring to include the national ideals of AKS into its party platform. It displays much of the spirit of the freedom wars, which guarantees the popularity among the youth, and thus its future growth. The party just put forward an economic policy liberal enough to allow large numbers of working-class farmers and workers behind it. Then, no human might can prevent their victory. And then the day shall finally come when the sun rises from behind de-Russified Karelian woods and Ingrian plains. These spring days are reminiscent of the time 14 years ago when the first platoons of youth made their way toward Prääzä. Crossing swamps and rivers during spring floods, they fought in Palalahti and Vieljärvi. On the ninth day, these troops of lads arrived, with their 22-year-old commander at Prääzä, well over a hundred kilometers from the Finnish border, at a crossroads, and from there, their path went on to Petrozavodsk and Lake Onega via Matrosy and Polovina.

Brothers in arms! Many years have passed since those days, with many comrades already made mute by the cloak of death. We are scattered across Finland, some of us outside the country. We are in different positions in our society, with different interests and priorities. But there is one thing we have in common: brotherhood in arms. The words of von Döbeln are true for us:

You shall see, that the bond forged in battle and danger, with blood and death, cannot ever be shattered. As such you and all of us are convinced of each other's love, for the brotherhood of arms is for life.

We are also reminded of the winter three years ago and the forest guerrillas at a fire guarding near the Kirov railway. Many a comrade remained there, hanging from the Russians' barbed wire or covered by Karelian dirt. I remember that as we dressed a comrade's wound or rubbed their frostbitten arm or leg with snow, we never mentioned political parties. There was only one, shall we say, patriotic national movement or youth movement, one that no one had mentioned to us, but whose call we heard in our hearts.

Much was sacrificed by that movement, things which many people in Finland still do not know. They were paid much more attention to in Moscow than in Helsinki. Once again we see fires reflected in the clouds gathering in the east. The near future will show if they signify the funeral pyre or a new beginning for Finland. May God forgive this nation, so that we may be one when the storm cloud of war finally arrives, and be able to bring the message of freedom all the way to the extreme end, where the last young guardsman who fell in the last Karelian war sleeps. Then the prayer of our national poet, given at the dawn of our freedom, will become true: "It is the dawn of Your victory that will allow Finland to be great!"

We Believe in the Future

NYKS[58] Flag Dedication Ceremony, October 20, 1933

It has been ten and a half years since the black flag of AKS was first raised. At the time the following words were spoken: "Our flag is as black as night, but after all, it is in a dark night that the shards of our tribe wonder ... but the sword of our faith and hatred strikes bright sparks in the night, predicting dawn."

Those of us who were standing then, under our newly consecrated flag, felt in our fiery youth that a new dawn for the Finnish tribe was just about to break. But there have been many bitter and heavy disappointments during the passing years. The iron ring of bloody terror has been wound ever tighter around our brother tribes of Karelia and Ingria. Tens of thousands of our tribal brethren have been struck down or forcibly carried off to starve in a distant wilderness. An Ingrian mother writes from the Siberian tundras, "The rest of us will die here. You never know when another one will perish. My little girl perished with her hand against her cheek. The martyr's crown is the one thing no one can steal from her."

But even so, we believe in the future, we believe in God, whose powerful arm will punish the guilty and allow justice to prevail. We are still young and will remain young, as we keep this faith in our hearts. The faith of youth is tremendous, capable of moving mountains. It is full of hope, and in times of national uncertainty, it will intuitively know what must be done, even if the calculations of those who believe in so-called *realpolitik* suggest

---

[58] NYKS (Naisylioppilaiden Karjala-Seura), "Female University Students' Karelia Association." As the name suggests this was a similar association to the AKS, but for female students.

otherwise.

Because of this, we believe in the resurrection of Karelia and Ingria, and we pray for it. We believe in the national awakening of the Finnish people, this people whose blood flows so thick and stiff. We continue working so that one day a smile will adorn the teary faces of Karelian and Ingrian mothers and that a morning sun over a free Karelia might shine on the graves of our comrades.

Along with the AKS, NYKS has always been there to maintain this faith among students and the Finnish people in general. With a typically feminine modesty and patience, they have contented themselves to carry out even mundane tasks that onlookers cannot see from the outside, and therefore they have not received praise for it, nor have they expected or demanded it. NYKS has carried out invaluable work along with AKS, and therefore it is with joy that AKS receives the flag of our sister organization among academic flags.

Members of NYKS! I consecrate this flag to its purpose. May it be a symbol for the burning love of the Fatherland, a courageous belief for the future, and a willingness to sacrifice of the NYKS members. May it be always seen flowing where our people are guided toward the shore of the coming Greater Finland. May God in his grace bless this flag, the ideals it represents, and the youth who follow it along the path of their newly awakened conscience.

The Land of Winds

15th Anniversary Celebration of the Estonian
Independence War, Helsinki, March 22, 1934.

It has been 15 years since Finnish volunteers fought their final battles in the Pechory front[59] in the Estonian freedom war. The suffering of the Pechory front ended the string of glorious victories for Finnish soldiers in Estonia. In early January 1919, the first of them arrived at the front. They fought and won. Among the victories won by the first Finnish battalion, the greatest were those of Lagena and Narva. The Finnish platoons took over Narva with a daring attack, taking the Russians by surprise, who could hardly believe their eyes when they saw Finnish bayonets gleaming in the night at Narva. *Krasnaya Gazeta*[60] wrote of this greatest act of heroism by the first Finnish Volunteer Corps[61] thus: "200 white guardsmen drove the Red Army, numbering in their thousands, out of Narva."

At the end of January, the Pohjan pojat[62] regiment arrived in Estonia, engaging in bloody battles on the Valk front. We saw the Pohjan pojat together with the Kuperjanov's guerrillas[63] spill their blood near the Paju Manor, we saw them wade through heavy snow, past enemy lines into Latvia and take over Marienburg. In between these large battles they carried out courageous ranger

---

[59] Pechory is a town in eastern Estonia, now in Russian territory.

[60] Krasnaya Gazeta ("The Red gazette"), a Communist party newspaper that was published in St. Petersburg.

[61] As the name suggests, the First Finnish Volunteer Corps was the first unit of Finnish volunteers formed to fight in the Estonian Independence War of 1918-19. It had a strength of about 1550 men.

[62] Pohjan pojat, literally "the sons of the north," were the second group of Finnish volunteers. Their strength was approx. 2200 men.

[63] Julius Kuperjanov (1894 – 1919) was a military leader during Estonia's war of Independence.

trips deep into enemy territory. Then, the arch of victory of the Finnish troops ended in the pointless but tenacious suffering of the Pechory front. The result of this war was the freedom of our southern brother people.

In these days many exclaim that the youth have no interest in political activism. To this, I would remind you how efficiently the Finnish youth were able to influence Estonian politics in 1919 — not to even mention our own freedom war. Their influence was outright decisive in Narva, the battle at the Paju Manor, and in Marienburg and in other bloody battles, in which hundreds of young Finnish lads gave their lives and sustained injuries that would leave them disabled for life, without asking for honor. To understand how much suffering, cold, hunger, blood, and tears those few months included, one has to have taken part in war himself. And remember, the youngest among them were only 13 or 14 years old. The Finnish volunteers asked for very little and received even less. The Finnish state had nothing it wished to say to these heroes, much less to assist them in any way. Because these Finnish heroes had been forgotten, AKS and other academic tribal associations planned a 15th anniversary celebration, as a meager gesture in their honor.

But due to external influences, this celebration's nature, atmosphere, and the colors we have it under are quite different from what was intended. We have received dismaying intelligence of the violence the Estonian establishment has resorted to in its attempts to quell the awakening movement led by their local veterans, a movement that is supported by a majority of the Estonian people. We have had to hear for months now, how the freedom warriors of Estonia must contend with an endless deluge of slanderous filth.

But now something that manages to shock even us, in these degraded times, has happened. The noblest leaders of the Estonian freedom fighters have been captured and thrown into dungeons, their organizations disbanded, and they have been denied even the most elemental civil rights. It is with the greatest distress that we must ask, was Estonia ready for the freedom that the Estonian people, supported by Finnish young volunteers, bought 15 years ago with their own blood?

The academic youth of Finland, along with all Finnish nationalists, must protest the actions of Estonia's power usurpers. The Vaps Movement[64] was perhaps too naive to believe their government's assurances of democracy, parliamentarism, and free elections. But that is absolutely the only mistake we can fault them for, and one they are paying a dear price for now. Of course, our domestic opponents here in Finland would forbid us to take part in the politics of other countries. But too much Finnish blood has been spilled in Estonia for us to not take an interest in the handling of a heritage that belongs, in a not insignificant part, also to Finnish heroes.

We are the comrades, parents, and family members of boys whose blood was spilled for the liberty of our tribal brothers. We are fully within our rights to demand the Estonian government to explain on what they base their accusations of treason toward our Estonian brothers in arms.

We have no right to criticize foreign leaders—so be it. But we have the right to ask: How do the Estonian usurpers plan to prove that such men as Sirk, Röuk, Dunkel, Kook, Jalakas, Mähar, and others now languishing in dungeons are supposedly guilty of treason against the nation they liberated from the hordes of Eastern barbarians, with their own blood?

We have the right to ask General Laidoner[65]: Will he really allow the prisoners to starve themselves to death, as they have begun a hunger strike as their last resort against this brutality? All this we demand to know, in the name of tribal brotherhood, humanity, and the brotherhood in arms formed in blood in Estonia in 1919. Finland's academic youth have successfully managed the relations with our southern brother nation

---

[64] The Vaps Movement was an association of veterans of the Estonian Independence War.
[65] General Johan Laidoner (1884-1953) was the commander-in-chief of the Estonian military in 1918, 1924 and 1934-1940.

throughout our independence. It will of course continue to do so, but unless we receive answers to these pressing questions, it is impossible to recognize Estonia's current rulers as the legitimate representatives of the Estonian people.

Sadly we know in advance, that such answers will not be forthcoming. It is with sympathy that we follow the Estonian veterans' struggle for their freedom and for the future of their people. This shameful stain on the contemporary history of Estonia will not be washed away until the ideals they represent have triumphed. Only then can we be confident that our tribal brethren have the ability to defend themselves against the threat from the Eastern steppes, which is always waiting for the opportunity to exterminate Estonia's freedom in fire and blood.

Despite everything, we believe in Estonia's future. A certain Estonian poet calls his nation the land of winds because harsh winds of destiny have constantly blown across their plains. Often Estonia has been in ruins and their people defeated almost down to the very last man. During the reign of Charles XII, mounted armies of Cossacks, Kalmyks, and Bashkirs made their way through Estonia, and the commander wrote to the czar: "Livonia[66] and most of Estonia are so empty that these places no longer exist, except on maps."

And still, the Estonian people have risen from ashes and blood. The chronicle of Estonian freedom cannot and will not end. The spirit of Estonian freedom fighters, the Kuperjanov guerrillas, lives on, and no arbitrary decrees or the darkness of dungeons can extinguish it. May our celebration here today send a message of hope across the Gulf of Finland: "We believe that justice will triumph, we believe in Estonia's future."

---

[66] Livonia is a historical territory which covered southern part of present-day Estonia and northern Latvia.

One Day, Karelia Shall be Free!

AVA 15th Anniversary Celebration, August 4, 1934

The officers who were to talk in this event were unable to attend because of—shall we say—reasons of *sensitivity*, to use an expression that is certainly not to be in breach of any laws limiting our speech. Also, the Jäger Major von Hertzen, who works as the local county doctor, has been detained, because as it happens, entirely by coincidence, of course, the head officer of the national medical institute happened to come by his post for an inspection.

So I will be here speaking in his stead, even though I would very much prefer to express my views with bayonets pointed toward the east. The memories of 15 years past have flooded back heavily in the last few days. At the time there was a group of lads here in Sortavala,[67] ready to depart toward an unknown fate. Among them were men who took part in the Freedom War, or the war in Estonia, but also young lads who were there for the first time. They were wide-eyed in wonder as they left for the trip, the end of which there would be no mercy given, nor asked for. The same wonder remained in their eyes even in death: why must I die?

They were the pioneers of the Greater Finland ideal, who spent their life's blood rushing toward the "rising shore of Finland."[68] The duration of the trip was to be two months, but many of them returned before that, mute and cold. They gave their lives with the same unselfish zeal, typical of youth.

Brothers in arms! We are now spread far and wide across the

---

[67] A village in Karelia, now within the Russian Olonetsky District.
[68] "rising shore of Finland" is a reference to the words of the Jäger March.

fatherland. But even so, we are one, for is it not true that brotherhood of warriors is for life. It remains among us, who were there to feel the rush of victory and the depression of defeat and who returned to carry our work in peacetime. And it also remains among those who left us to join the army of the unseen. Above all, we remember you, our former commanding officers, many of whom are attending this ceremony. I am one of your soldiers. I wish to thank you on behalf of all of us. You were not promoted; you were not rewarded. But please know that we, your former soldiers, have not forgotten you, and we never will.

It has been asked, why did it have to happen the way it did? Why was blood spilled in vain? Russia was on the brink of collapse. If only we had received a little more support, the border would have been pushed to where it should be, at the river Svir.

Different government cabinets have been blamed. Why did Finland not seize its opportunity? Why was the battle at Polovina, which opened the way to Petrozavodsk, not followed by a final strike which would have crushed the enemy? Why did the government not prevent the catastrophe at Vitele? In my opinion, the government cannot be blamed, for each people have the kind of government they deserve. Instead, we must search for the reason among the people and ask why there was no consensus that giving necessary support for active efforts is necessary. The people of Finland are still not fully awake to the fact that we are the final guardians of the heritage of our peoples, here in the farthest north. It has not awakened to demand what is theirs: a free Karelia joined with Finland! Similarly, the cause of Karelia will perish, if this awakening does not take place. We have lost our faith in political parties, after all the dealings we have seen them engaging in, in the buying and selling of the Fatherland. Only a vigorous nationalist awakening can create a sense of national will that can lead to Karelian freedom one day. The Karelian question is, of course, ultimately in the hands of the Karelians themselves, but it is also a matter of an expansionist Finnish movement, with the ultimate goal of creating a great

Finnish nation in the North. This revivalism must be carried out so that it grabs the Finnish people in their entirety. Once this is achieved, we will have advanced our goals to the point where they can no longer be stopped.

Meeting old, scarred comrades, one feels that we are in agreement in this: "the guard may fall, but not surrender." We did not surrender in the war, so we will not surrender now! No matter the storm of political infighting around us, we must not surrender. For our work remains unfinished. The whispered promise we made, as we dug graves for fallen comrades in the distant Karelian wilderness, remains unfulfilled. We must remember — always remember — the lad whose watch there is now eternal. We must fight to advance the Karelian cause ceaselessly, even if with different weaponry, on different fronts than in 1919.

In fact, a battle of this sort may be more taxing to us, who are more used to making our arguments with rifles and bayonets. Nevertheless, we are, and we must be prepared to fight! This is a decision each one of us must make individually. It should not be done while reading a newspaper, not while listening to agitators, but while listening to one's own conscience. And once we find our solution, we must stick to it no matter what. We must not relinquish it to any authority. The only thing that gives one the required strength to do this is an unwavering belief in the eventual resurrection of the Finnish people, which will also be the resurrection of Karelia and Ingria.

Yesterday, we heard a song of lamentation from the banquet hall. We no longer hear them from Karelia itself — there are no more tears to be shed there. They have waited for the dawn for too long and have been disappointed too many times. But one day, geopolitics may take a promising turn. A tense situation may begin unraveling and with the buzz of bombers. Then it will be time for AVA[69] men to understand that for once the Finnish people must take the opportunity they have been given. With my

---

[69] AVA (Aunuksen vapaaehtoinen armeija, "Olonets Voluntary Army")

trust in this, I should like to shout over the barbed-wire fences toward the land of our youthful dreams, Olonets: "Wait just a bit longer, our ranks are growing!" I want to shout so loud, that even our comrades resting underground can hear it: "Soon we will depart again! You did not die in vain! One day Karelia shall be free!" Let us pray that the Lord will permit it tomorrow!

For a Finnish University

Parliamentary Remarks, January 24, 1935

The university question is a Finnish, and solely a Finnish, issue. It is an issue for a nation that is becoming a Finnish ethnostate. Such a state must — despite the propaganda distortions of our own homegrown Swedish minority — find its own place in the sun that historically belongs to any independent and forward-thinking people. A fully Finnish university is an absolute necessity to safeguard higher intellectual civilization in Finland. Our leftists make a mistake in saying that it is irrelevant to argue whether there are one or two Swedish-speaking tenured professors in the university. The question is whether we manage to create an entirely Finnish university, Finnish not only in its spirit but in its language.

If a Finnish university has Swedish-minded instructors, who do not consider our people their own, do not understand their soul and mentality, and lack the sense of being Finns and the idea of the Finnish people's role in history, how can they instill in their students the sense of nationalism they need, in order for them to become the Fatherland's new hope? For as long as Finnish professors and docents work alongside Swedish-speaking ones, a sense of discrepancy will remain in our institutes of higher learning, and this will cause permanent disagreements and conflict.

There are legitimate forms of patriotism. The Finnish people have always had too little of those. But once they awaken, they will demand for themselves the only truly Finnish university in the world. They will not feel equal among other peoples for as long as they do not have this institution that upholds higher civilization. Especially since our independence, this requirement has been more and more obvious for it to continue to nourish the holy flame that—as incredible as this may seem—continues to burn in the breast of Finnish university students. It is incredible because they have received their education from Swedish-minded instructors, whose attitude toward their nationalist ideals has been cold, indifferent, even hostile.

I am convinced that not since the times of Snellman has there been such a nationalist fervor among university students. It is not surprising that this fervor sometimes takes somewhat excessive forms. Even so, they are still surely more proper and serious than among the university youth of other nations.

The University of Helsinki will soon celebrate its 300th anniversary. The time for the national dream of a truly Finnish university has come. This desire has gained in force and seriousness for a university that can cherish and develop the most important inheritance of Finnish culture and continue to do so in a Finnish ethnostate.

The outrageous methods of the current political elite, which have been the subject of much discussion here, have created a necessary and unavoidable reaction. And the reaction is not limited to students, but among the general population, there is also a widespread nationalist awakening taking place. Its scope and significance are too great to understand from the present perspective. The historical importance of the present developments will only be understood in the future. For many years I assumed that our national character was in permanent torpor, due to the daily insults from our Swedish minority, which we refused to react to, no matter how outrageous they became. However, now the psychological moment has come, one which is very rare in the history of nations, and one which we must therefore hold onto—the moment of Finnish nationalist uprising.

This came as a surprise to those who then began to attempt to dampen the righteous pursuit of the Finnish people, even if this is in conflict with the constitution and laws. However, the triumph of the Finnish spirit cannot be prevented any longer — this includes also the university issue. I should like our Swedes and their supporters to realize that this battle is lost. The rise of the Finnish ethnostate is a fact that surely they too can finally see, and their attempts to slow the process will only create bitterness and resentment, which in turn will weaken the entire people. A Finnish university will become a reality, as an expression of the present nationalist spirit!

Before the Fatherland

Parliamentary Remarks, January 24, 1935

Our country's Constitutional Law Committee has agreed to the removal of mandatory membership in a student nation. In addition, they have even suggested that the membership in the students' union would be made voluntary.

One would think that being aware of similar changes made in other countries, they would hesitate to step onto this slippery slope. Membership in a nation and students' union means that our academic citizens are being brought up to become responsible citizens in our society, based on legality, and to learn the duties of a citizen in such a society. A university student cannot refuse to join a nation any more than a regular citizen can refuse to pay taxes. Just as a citizen cannot decide whether they wish to obey the law or not, it is equally preposterous if membership in the miniature societies formed by students were to became voluntary.

The student union, its membership numbering in the thousands, runs the risk of becoming corrupted by impropriety if the discipline exercised by the student nation were to be removed. At a time when our youth face many temptations, one would think that the state would be concerned with fortifying, rather than destroying, the discipline the nations have successfully exercised among our students for three centuries. The view of the Swedish-minded is easy to understand since they are aware of the Finnish nationalist spirit growing in the student nations and the work being done to create a Finnish ethnic state and to remove the privileges of the Swedes. It has always been the student nations that have been the forerunners of nationalist awakening, and their honor rolls include such names as J.V. Snellman, Arwidsson,[70] Elias Lönnrot, Yrjö Koskinen, Agathon Meurman, Danielson-Kalmari, and many others.[71]

A young student's bright mind and strong will direct him to take an active stance on matters that he instinctively understands are crucial to the fate of Fatherland. Were this not the case, and if our students were not acutely expressing their opinions, or sincerely searching for their own views, by taking part in the discussions at meetings on every level, in the press and among different citizens' associations, this would be a sign of a moribund country and people. What use does the Fatherland have for youth who do not search for truth, do not see great, noble national vistas and goals, not to mention have the courage to speak out their ideas and convictions, once they have reached them, even at the risk of ridicule or condemnation? What would the Fatherland do with youth who consider their own selfish needs more weighty on the scale than the whole?

The suggestion of removing the mandatory membership in nations comes from those who do not understand the active nationalism and fighting spirit of today's youth. The assault against this institution and those behind it deserves to be classified as negative-minded and desirous of creating confusion and disunity. The point of this attack is directed at the very finest elements of our academic youth. The critique unfortunately cannot be expressed in milder terms than this. Some mystifying ideas have been uncovered. Because students are involving themselves in politics, the whole institution of student unions must perish. And from this preposterous idea we go on to conclude that if it is not necessary for a student to belong to a nation, he does not need to be a member of the student union, either. The attempt is to strip the nations of their power, foolishly

---

[70] Adolf Ivar Arwidsson (1791-1858) was a Finnish nationalist political journalist, writer and historian

[71] Yrjö Sakari Yrjö-Koskinen (born Georg Zakarias Forsman, 1830- 1903), Agathon Meurman (1826-1909), and Johan Richard Danielson-Kalmari (1853 – 1933) were all important figures in the Fennoman movement.

believing that this will erase the patriotic feeling of their members. Therefore, they wish to remove the financial support of membership fees from the nations, and thus, the attackers hope to reduce the nations' membership by as much as possible. They wish to render the nations insignificant, or preferably altogether dead, simply because nationalist students form the majority in their membership, and this is anathema to those who wish to remove the nations. They wish to destroy, or to at least dilute and corrupt the new life force of Finnish nationalism, which gains ground among students year by year with the unstoppable force of truth. They wish to remove this most central idea of any organized society, which supposedly governs our state as well, that is, that a minority cannot dictate to the majority.

It would be a mistake not to expose, directly and without whitewashing the truth, the real motives of those who wish to destroy the institution of student nations here and now. What drives them? Is it a fault, that nations' activities are characterized by a strong love of one's home region, the Fatherland, and a sacrificing awareness of the tribal question? If education, when it is carried out with this sort of mentality, is politicking, then yes, the student nations are certainly to be considered guilty both when it comes to their internal activities, as well as those in which they interact with society at large.

Student nations' gatherings and celebrations are fueled by a strong love for one's home, fatherland, the entire Finnic tribe. And these three influences are obvious in all the activities they undertake which are visible to outsiders. If these factors, which seem to cause so much grief to some, were to either be eliminated or diluted to a degree that the internationalist finds acceptable — one that carries out no actual work and sacrifices nothing for the good of the Fatherland — would the educational task of the nations lose all of its meaning? The nations fund the travel of delegations of students each summer so that they may travel to their home regions, to the silents woods, and to give lectures to the common folk, who thirst for knowledge. Week after week, they study the life of our people, for the good of science, and under the guidance of science, in order to bring back new, valuable additions to the sum total of our knowledge of ourselves.

It is the flame of love for one's Fatherland, lit and maintained by the student nation, that gives purpose to the members of such delegations. Anyone who thinks that when the nations send their members on these expeditions, they equip them with arrogance and suspicion toward the less fortunate, is utterly mistaken. Every university student understands his social responsibility and is fully capable of gaining the trust of a wilderness dweller. And I can assure you that the sense of solidarity among the student nations, as well as the entirely nationalist student body, is now stronger than ever before. It is due to the so-called incitement that makes bureaucrats recoil and wish to destroy, at all costs and by any means possible.

Finland's university students believe in greater Finland, each generation of them more so than the one before. For older folk, it may be a beautiful dream, which they do not feel can become a reality. For students, it is a part of their worldview; it is a part of their flesh and blood. Students are attracted to the tribal cause because they understand its end goal is a greater, more powerful, and whole Finland. Would the idea of passive and active resistance in the years of oppression, or the idea of Finnish independence, have survived without the students to carry them forward?

It can be said that the Jäger movement, too, had its origins in the student nations. Finland would have been unable to cut itself off from the giant to the east when the right moment arrived, if it wasn't for the youth who defied the wise and the cautious, by sending their best to Germany. The Jäger movement is the laurel wreath of the nations, and no amount of violence can remove it, even if the nations themselves are destroyed. Our people are so young as a civilized nation, that we cannot afford to defile the few historical traditions that we do have. We must honor them instead. The youth have, always have had, and must have the right to take part in politics, when it is done for the Fatherland. No one can deny them this right, since it is based on the purity and sincerity of their patriotism, in a sincere search for truth and the clarity of youth. Who can claim that they had ever been mistaken when they acted in the best interest of the Fatherland and its future?

Removing mandatory membership in a student nation may bankrupt some of them. But it will not erase the patriotic and nationalist spirit that shines so brightly that it disturbs eyes blinded by class hatred or internationalism. Not even the parliament can deprive our students of this. They stand as a wall protecting the fatherland, defiant, steadfast, believing in *Finnish* civilization and education, believing also that one day the Finnish people, including the working class, will create a Finnish ethnostate.

The Face of the New Youth

Sinimustat (Blue-Black) Organization Rally,
Heimola Hall, April 8, 1935

Some days ago a certain newspaper published a letter from a reader, who wrote under the pseudonym "An Old Man." In his piece, this "old man" related his experiences of the youth of his hometown. He said that he found them degenerate and that obscenities and curses constantly flowed from their lips. A few days later, in the same paper, another reader writing under the pseudonym "A Blue-Black's Mother" responded to "An Old Man," suggesting he attend this meeting in Heimola, to have the opportunity to see the other face of Finland's youth.

I do hope that "An Old Man" took the advice offered to him. Here he could see the youth, whose face can instill in anyone a belief in a future for the people of Finland, even in these trying times. This face was lost for a long time, during the reaction to the freedom war. The face of Finland's youth was curiously distorted during that time, by the curse of base desires and class hatred. Those who hold the future of this country and people dear to their hearts almost despaired at our youth.

But little by little a new awakening began to make its way into the soul of our youth. Once again, it began to brighten up and resemble the face we had seen in the days of the freedom war and tribal wars. The face we saw, tearing up and pressed against mother's shoulder in the moment of departure. The face we had seen glowing with vigor while rushing toward fire and death. The face that was never more beautiful than when resting, pale and serene, on the cushions inside a white casket.

The same purity begins to again spread on the face of our

youth now, at the time of a national awakening. As soon as it spreads on the face of all of our youth, our dream of a greater Fatherland will be a reality. This is the other face of Finland's youth, and upon looking at them, "An Old Man" could not possibly despair.

Some wonder why so many youth gather around the IKL flag. The reason is simply that this movement for youth awakening has to offer the ideals without which they will be ideologically starved. Youth, in their teenage years especially, desire ideological guidance and high principles, something to strive for, and battle. In this sense, political parties are holding an empty goblet to the lips of someone dying of thirst. They cannot offer the youth any high ideals, even if the bourgeois parties do base their activities on a patriotic ideal. The ideal of freedom is the high ideal, which the youth of any age has always believed in and fought for. It has always fought against oppression and violence, no matter where and in which area of life and society it may appear. Always, where the struggle has been for the freedom of thought and religion, national sovereignty, have youth been in the forefront. This freedom struggle can be suppressed for generations, the youth can be defeated to the last man, their banner can be trampled into the mud.

But the ideal of freedom is indestructible, and it is always passed on to the next generation; a new generation rises to follow in the footsteps of the previous defeated generation. It lifts up the flag from the ground and carries on the unfinished work of the previous generations, carrying it on to victory. The youth who have been swept away by this new nationalist worldview believe they are fighting for the ideal of national freedom. This movement for national liberation wants to rid Finland of foreign race and of alien culture, political parties, party leaders, and career politicians. It wishes to liberate the Finnish working people of Marxism, from the slavery of Marxist overlords, and wishes to carry out societal righteousness toward the working class and the poor. It wishes to finish the battle for the freedom of the Karelian and Ingrian peoples, in this horrifying century of slavery and enforced peace treatises. This is the liberation movement of Finland's youth; this is its version of liberalism, one that is truly righteous and noble, a liberalism fitting of youth.

We have been accused of exaggeration and appeals to emotion. The same accusation has been wielded countless times toward the German youth of today as well. A certain culturally liberal Swedish magazine recently wrote of German youth today: "The youth of Germany have a frightening and morbid passion to sacrifice themselves for the greatness of Germany."

This passion, which the Swedish liberal considers frightening, even sickly, is the passion of every youth freedom movement. It is a pure and noble passion, and once embraced it will burn out any lower and base instincts that govern the hearts of many of our youth, as well. With this passion, the people of Germany have freed themselves of the Marxist curse, of the shackles of the enforced peace of Versailles, and now Germany marches, with its youth in front, toward a new time of greatness. This passion should fill the hearts of Finland's youth, along with the desire to sacrifice oneself, to give one's all for the Fatherland. Finland's youth aim so high that they must have a burning, fanatical belief, all the force and will of youth. We who lead this youth have been accused of permitting this type of incitement among the youth. Not only do we permit it, we carry it out systematically, so that this people may finally awaken.

Yet again is it said that this youth consists of nothing but a collection of "numbered plates," devoid of individual will. This they say of the first movement in history to stress the importance of individual personality. The popular will, such as it is in our country today, actually fears that a personality that is stronger than others will rise out of the mass. This is why so-called democracy sets its own strengths in motion to push that personality back into the background. We stress the value of individual personality, we wish to cultivate it in each person, so that they may become a person of true conscience. But we also demand that if someone has the qualities of a leader, he must be given the opportunity to use them, for the betterment of the people.

Never has the mass majority caused history to progress, only individual personalities, and their followers grouped around them with the binds of loyalty. This does not mean that the individuals loyal to the leader are mere puppets. The youth who fought in the freedom war and tribal wars were far from puppets, despite having leaders. The martyred youth Marjoniemi, who confessed that he had come to liberate Karelia when threatened with burning at a stake on the plains of Kiimäsjärvi, was as far from a puppet as possible. Young Pesonen, who fell for the freedom of Estonia with "Fatherland" as his last word, was no puppet. Let the man who would call these youth and their many heroic comrades "puppets" come forward!

And present-day youth follow in their footsteps. During the wake of one such martyred youth, when the entire congregation bathed in tears, the youth's mother began the hymn, "Praise the righteous Lord..." She thanked the Lord that she did not have to give birth to a puppet, but had the privilege of carrying under her heart a child, who could sacrifice his all for the freedom of an entire people. As long as mothers such as her are among this nation, generations of heroes will not die out, nor must we despair of our future. As long as new generations follow in the footsteps of Marjoniemi, Pesonen, and so many others, we believe in the liberation of Karelia and Ingria. For as long as the ranks of Blue-Black youth grow, we look to the future with faith and confidence. A new national, and along with it, religious awakening, is striking through the ranks of Finland's youth. The new youth rise like dew from the dawn of nationalist awakening. We hear those youth sing, we see their face, and we believe in the future greatness of the Fatherland.

The Path of Our Youth

IKL Rally, Helsinki, September 15, 1935

The path for our youth, guided by our new ideology, has been called a dangerous path. It has been said that down that path our youth will lose that which is most precious to them, that is, *freedom*. We cannot possibly understand, how we supposedly have sought to deprive our youth of their freedom. We have not forced anyone to join our ranks. Those who have joined us have done so because their conscience demands it.

The only freedom our message opposes is the freedom to live a degenerate and indulgent life. If the liberalism of our day wished to grant this type of freedom to our youth, then we would deprive them of it. For as long as the way is open for this type of "freedom" for our youngsters, they are in danger of falling into the most abject slavery that a human being can find himself in: the slavery of sin.

It is our claim that despite, or rather precisely because of this, our present youth movement is a movement for liberation. The Blue-Black youth is just as inspired by the ideal of freedom as any other previous generation. This youth movement wishes to fight for Finland's national freedom until it has all the freedoms that rightfully belong to it — from the university to the most primitive cabin in the wilderness. It desires to fight for the Finnish working class to liberate it from the slavery of Marxism. It wishes to do what it can to liberate Karelia and Ingria. Is this not enough of a freedom movement for one generation?

The Blue-Black youth has begun to carry out, both in word and in deed, the "propaganda of action." The same that our present prime minister once suggested we adopt, when during his youth he nearly fell into despair, when the attempts to Finnicize the universities failed. He wrote in *Raatajassa*[72] in 1907: "The Parliament shall do what it can; that which they cannot or will not do is our task, not with cowardly theories, but with a strong propaganda of action."

I mentioned that our youth also wish to advance the cause of Karelia and Ingria. I will take this opportunity to say a few words regarding the fate of our tribal siblings. We have been accused of creating a war psychosis in the youth and of planning an offensive war against Russia in order to take over Karelia and Ingria. Those who make these claims are either unfamiliar with our proclamations or are guilty of distorting the truth. We do understand that an army so badly equipped as the Finnish cannot possibly entertain the idea of defeating the world's most powerful military force. We know that for now, our active force differs from the army of Abyssinia only in that at least, in the Abyssinian army, each man has his own spear. And yet, here we can afford to allow a publication such as "Rauhaa kohti"[73] magazine. Still, we can afford to permit the spread of nihilistic peace propaganda. They bring all the way from Norway Nobel laureate "apostles of peace," as if we did not have enough of them already!

The youth, who may at any moment be called upon to defend our country, accuses the political parties and their leaders of bickering over power for 17 years and in the process, neglect to arm our military at this critical moment. And because of this, I will take the liberty of directing a few words to the party leaders of our country. Should the catastrophe happen, these young men will come back from their graves if necessary, to shout their mute accusations at you, for sending them unarmed against the best armed military force in the world. What do you answer to them at this moment, when the flames of a global conflagration can be seen on the horizon? Although at the moment a military intervention on behalf of our kindred peoples is out of the

---

[72] "The Drudge," a leftwing weekly published 1904–1910.
[73] "Toward Peace," a pacifist magazine.

question, we have also failed to use the internationally accepted peaceful methods. Finland's government was among the first to accept Soviet Russia into the League of Nations. When students concerned with the fate of our kindred people asked the then-prime minister, "What are the guarantees that the cause of Karelia and Ingria would be addressed in the League of Nations?", the prime minister answered that this issue is just as important to the government as it is to the students. We are still waiting for this promise to be fulfilled in actual deeds.

The latest news says that Finland's foreign minister has held a long speech in the League on the issue of Abyssinia. But we have an unarmed Abyssinia closer to us than Africa, we have a Karelia and Ingria, on whose behalf the minister of the exterior has not once opened his mouth. We have also waited in vain for the parliament to act. It is telling that when the geopolitical publication *Journal de Geneve* published their alarming report on the destruction taking place in Karelia and Ingria, we were too occupied with arguing over whether the Swedish-speaking MP's need a third interpreter or not. Last spring when we heard the information on the latest deportations in Ingria, we had our next to last session. In that session, the parliament decided to grant millions to build an embassy in Moscow, a location where no other bourgeois nation has their own embassy.

And now it has happened that Russia has rejected the building because its design was in the functionalist style. I suppose it is a fair question to ask: Is it really necessary to dwell on matters like this? It is indeed necessary so that the ideas of the Finnish people and the Finnish youth do not become confused, as they say, since it was stated today, "The politics of Europe are presently led by a man who wrote the book, *The Antichrist.*" Before the eyes of civilized Europe, the bloody ghosts of Karelia and Ingria make their way toward the wilderness of Afghanistan and Tuskertan, and the highest seat in the League of Nations is occupied by a man with the Jewish name Wallack-Meer.

And the only countries in the world where the present rulers of Russia are not to be mocked are the Soviet Union and Finland. Presently there is a massive fear of our youth turning fascist. If by fascism they mean the nationalist awakening which leads them to fight for a new nation and a new society, well that fear is indeed well-founded. No matter how hard our enemies may be, the youth already has become fascist, if you will, in the sense that they fight for a society that is freed of class hatred. The greatest mission of youth, as well as our entire movement, is to win back the soul of the working people for the Fatherland. To achieve this, no sacrifice can be too great and no agenda too radical. It is the resolution of this issue that will decide whether the people of Finland stand or fall.

Allow me to return to where I started, the speech by the foreign minister. He said, for example: "The present-day youth think that a perfect nation is possible, that the state in which the nation is everything and the individual is nothing is a happy state." It is indeed possible, and we believe it a happy state, where the individual is nothing, but the nation, the Fatherland, is all.

Hitherto the individual has meant too much, and the Fatherland, far too little. I have given the topic of my talk: the way of new youth. What is such a way? It is the way where the single person is meaningless, but the Fatherland means everything. What party do this youth support? They recognize the only political cause, that of the fatherland. We have seen such youth before in this country, and therefore we know it is possible again. What did the individual person mean compared to Fatherland, to the Jägers who departed for Germany? Or for the youth who fought in the battlefields of our freedom war, Karelia, and Ingria? Such is the path for our present youth, who follow our Blue-Black banner. Obviously, it is necessary to nevertheless humbly admit, that the perfect nation or the possibility of a perfect nation is not down here or on Earth. It can be achieved only there, the heavenly kingdom, where nothing is flawed or imperfect. The Lord has stated, of that kingdom: "My kingdom is not of this world." The youth who follow the path of love for the Fatherland in this world must never forget this. This Fatherland is only for bringing up our youth for the higher, heavenly Fatherland, and thus it is above everything else here on this mortal plane. Let this become clear to this organization, among whose ranks "the Blue-Blacks now march steadily in line."

"No One Who Puts a Hand to the Plow and Looks Back Is Fit"

AKS Oath Ceremony, December 6, 1935

Thus, the Lord addressed his disciples who had joined Him on his path toward the heavenly city above.

My fellow AKS members: are you on this same path toward the same city? We all walk toward eternity. When a prophet in the Old Testament asked the Lord: "What shall I preach?" the Lord replied, "All flesh is like grass, and all its glory like the flowers of the field; the grass withers and the flowers fall." We all are traveling toward eternity, but how many of us remember this in everyday life, and how many are consciously planning for their soul's salvation? If we are traveling somewhere, our faces must be turned toward the destination and with our back to where we started from. If we are making our way toward eternal life, we must always be facing in that direction and turn our back to everything that burdens us, to sin, and to the kind of life that makes us lose our souls. When the Lord said these words, someone came to Him and wished to follow him, but he asked first to say goodbye to his family at home. This the Lord did not permit. He said that those who would follow him must depart immediately and with no doubts. He said, "No one who puts a hand to the plow and looks back is fit." No one who would walk the straight and narrow path that leads to life must stay behind in order to say his goodbyes. When the Lord said this to the young man, He meant that if you go to your former comrades in sin, they will try to lure you back to it. You must not look behind, and you must depart immediately.

This message is for every one us of because every one of us is an eternal being. We all have been called by the Lord to follow Him. The call may have come in different ways, in different moments: at nighttime silence, in pain in a hospital bed, standing at the casket of a loved one. But we all have received the call, and now we must ask ourselves, have we answered and begun to follow Him?

As the spiritual call must be followed unequivocally, so it is with here, in the mortal realm. He who hears the Fatherland's call must stand before the teary face of the Fatherland and receive one of those tears into his own soul. It is a divine call. He who hears it must follow it and not look back, not ask anyone's permission, forget his own benefits, sacrifice his own future, and abandon all. Because the Fatherland's call, the call of the Fatherland that is down here, is also so great that it demands absolute obedience and commitment. When the Jägers heard this call, they departed and did not look back. Their fate was literally the same as the demand made by Jesus to the young man. They could not stop by home to make their goodbyes. They had to abandon their homes, their future, abandon everything, with no hesitation, without looking back. Those young men who fought in the freedom wars of Finland, Estonia, and Karelia often had to leave in secret, because they were following God rather than man. They could not hesitate for a moment. They had to burn all bridges behind them. They departed on their path, asking for nothing, promising to give everything. Today a group of AKS brothers stands under our flag, ready to give their oath.

The AKS flag is a battle flag, for AKS is an association for battle. Those who do battle must not stand still, ever. They must be constantly moving forward, and all its members must do their duty with no hesitation. The battle that we and Finland's nationalist youth are engaged in is brutal. We fight for the cause of Ingria and Karelia at a time when they would silence those who wish to express their distress. We fight for a new society, for a new country. We fight for societal righteousness. We fight for a system that can create a strong nation. This struggle is often nerve-wracking, more so than an actual war, because the individual in this fight must abandon his ordinary quiet life. He may lose his peace of mind in this struggle. His nerves may wear thin. The candle of his life may burn out all too soon. This is no play war.

So pause, AKS brothers, before your own conscience and take a moment to consider: how is it that you depart for this fight? How have you already taken part in it? You may be excited to take part. You may be talented. You have all the external and internal qualities that a member of AKS requires. But do you still lack concern for your own soul or the souls of others? Do you see souls in distress around you? Does the sea of sin heaving around you burn your own soul too? The degeneracy in which you see Finland's youth sinking into? Does the downfall of other AKS members sting your soul, when you see a young member depart for student life, full of faith, and then see that faith extinguished? When you see some internal illness eating him from within, draining his mind and his soul, dulling his bright eyes, and erasing the purity and faith of youth from his face and personality. You know then that life in Helsinki has begun to corrupt the eager lad. You know that inner instincts, the drive to commit sin, are severing the roots of life. Here, in the midst of busy life that drains the best energies of youth, the faith of childhood vanishes and the tears of his mother and father are forgotten. For us to be true men of the AKS, the reality of this must be a heavy burden. We must have the same mindset as Paul, who said, "Who is weak, and I do not feel weak? Who is led into sin, and I do not inwardly burn?"

Therefore, AKS brother, remember what the righteous man said to the father of the Awakening movement, "You lack only one thing, and because of that you lack everything: an internal sense of Christ."

I have seen it as my duty to speak to you about this, AKS brothers, because my mind has been too preoccupied by the sinfulness, the sinfulness of university students, the moral distress of our youth. Whoever feels the concern for them cannot but pray that a spiritual awakening would come, along with the nationalist one. In our country's history, spiritual and nationalist awakenings have often gone side by side. During the war of 1714-1721, when the remains of our people began to repopulate this land after withstanding horrors, the spiritual awakening spread quickly among the rising people. During the time of J. V. Snellman, a religious movement worked alongside his nationalist work. I am convinced that if a similar religious awakening does not renew our present youth, our nationalist youth from within, we shall never achieve the great goal we have sworn to fight for. We need not only rousing speeches, men of outstanding talent, tireless organizers, and political fighters; we need men who have been reborn from the inside and who will in turn begin to renew this country and its life from the inside. But for as long as this does not happen, we must lament as Jeremiah did for the defeat of his people: "Oh, that my head were a spring of water and my eyes a fountain of tears! I would weep day and night for the slain of my people!"

Brothers of the AKS! I know that you understand what I am talking about. I am convinced that if we look into our conscience as we stand before our flag, we all must mourn our own weakness, our spiritual sickness, all our neglected duties. This includes us older AKS men, for we have sinned so gravely against God, the Fatherland, and each other, that without forgiveness we shall be utterly lost. If only God in his mercy may allow that to happen in the midst of our people obsessed with entertainment and enslaved by the lowest impulses, the present youth may finally make the dream of our heroic dead a reality. Above all, it was the dream of Bobi Sivén, whom we remember every time our flag is raised and we honor the lads who once departed without looking back.

The true honor guard of the AKS flag are the ghosts of these heroes. We must remain a strong and united group as we follow their footsteps. It is the AKS and the Blue-Blacks who personify the great promise for the future of the Fatherland and its people. For their sake, we must bend the knee before God. For their own sake, we must tell them to trust, no matter how much it may sting. We lay such a heavy burden on their youthful shoulders so that it drives them to truly fight their way into the future. Without this burden and this sorrow, our own speeches mean nothing, for they are nothing but "only a resounding gong or a clanging cymbal." Without it, our troops cannot penetrate the obstacles on their path. Brothers of the AKS about to swear your oath and those of us who once swore the same oath, remember that, "No one who puts a hand to the plow and looks back is fit."

The Demands of Our National Honor

Parliamentary Remarks, December 4, 1936

I would like to draw your attention to the deportations currently widely carried out among the people of Karelia and Ingria by the Soviet Union. By doing so, The Soviet Union crassly breaks the agreements and responsibilities it took upon itself in the Tarto peace agreement regarding Karelia and Ingria, agreements which the other parties have followed to the letter. The Tarto treaty promised the Karelians national sovereignty and autonomy, and the Ingrians cultural autonomy. It is obvious that with these actions, the Soviet Union breaks and continues to break the treaty. In 1929 the deportations began in Eastern Karelia. Then many trains loaded with deportees were taken to the Kola peninsula or the mines or forests of Siberia. The deportations reached a peak in 1931, then stopped after 1931, beginning again in 1935. At that time many Ingrians were taken to Turkestan, Tashkent, and Almaty. During this year most deportations have been to areas east of Leningrad (St. Petersburg), especially the area of Vologda.

The deportees live in the most miserable conditions imaginable, without even basic necessities. Because of this, their mortality rate is extremely high, especially among children. If they are not helped soon, they will become practically extinct. 50,000 Ingrians have been deported up to date, and a slightly smaller number of Karelians. Finland's foreign ministry must pay more attention to this situation. Our government must understand that it has certain responsibilities toward our kindred peoples and that it must find a way to carry out these responsibilities. Especially now we have the opportunity to do just that, since the Soviet Union has joined the League of Nations, the institution in which our foreign minister places so much stock. In the founding document of the League, it is said expressly that a nation that wishes to join it must give assurances that it intends to carry its international duties sincerely. However, the Soviet Union made it known, before its membership became the subject of deliberation, that it would not accept any pronouncements regarding matters that took place before they joined the League.

However, France and England refused to accept this explanation in the political committee that was preparing the membership accord of the Soviet Union, and Finland, in voting for the membership, announced it was doing so with the assumption that in its membership the Soviet Union takes upon itself to comply with its international treaties, according to the founding document of the League. Foreign minister Hackzell even held a notably long speech regarding this matter in the League.

The Soviet Union has broken international treaties and continues to do so now. I must ask the government if they intend to remain entirely silent on this question, even as this national tragedy has attracted international attention. Our previous government at least did not take any significant action. When a delegation of students some years previously visited the then foreign minister to demand answers — during the decisive phase of the Soviet Union entering the League of Nations — and expressed their view that it had been left to languish, the prime minister replied that in his view the government had done their duty and that he was happy to report that his conscience was completely clean, when it comes to East Karelia.

He went on to say that he had no idea when the matter might be discussed in the League of Nations. We no longer have the opportunity to turn to the cabinet, the prime minister of which so forcefully felt his obligations toward Karelia. However, we do wish to address the present cabinet and ask them whether it has made any plans to act at all. The previous government's only concrete action was — if I am not mistaken on this matter — a protest in the form of a question regarding the deportations. The USSR replied shortly that this is an internal matter and is of no concern to anyone else. This was the reply with which Finland found itself having to contend. However, the view that this was only an internal matter pertaining to the Soviet Union is clearly and unquestionably false. Let us remind ourselves what the foremost experts on international law stated in 1923, regarding Karelia. I have no time, nor the opportunity, at this moment to rephrase them in detail. Our current foreign minister knows them better anyway. However, these experts on legal matters were of the opinion that it is not merely an internal matter for the Soviet Union, but rather that Finland has the right to enforce the agreements mandated by articles 10 and 11 of the Tarto peace treaty and their corresponding declarations. As examples of the international attention these deportations have attracted, let me mention that many notable international magazines have published articles on the issue, such as *Journal de Geneve* and *Times*.

The matter was also discussed at length at the National Socialist party's Nurnberg rallies. Especially binding, from the point of view of the Finnish government, is an article by the prestigious Swedish magazine, *Nya Dagligt Allehandan* titled, "Sweden must not remain Silent." The article contains the following words, addressed clearly, straight at the Finnish government: "This matter of course pertains most pertinently to Finland."

It is now up to the Finnish government to decide to which extent they can now continue the talks that were started in Geneva in 1921 and 1922, which have so far been fruitless. All experts in international law remarked at the time that the Soviet assurances are binding. Allow us to remind you now that this places each member of the League not only in a legally, but also morally binding position. The vice-president of Switzerland, Guiseppe Motta, wished to emphasize these moral obligations when he said, "Now that the delegates are in Geneva, we hope that voices will be raised for the sake of humanity. That explanation will be demanded from their government, an explanation for the anti-religious propaganda that has no precedent in human history and which makes anyone who believes in God and prays for his righteousness weep."

This is the view of a nation that voted against allowing the Soviet Union in the League, unlike Finland. To our foreign minister: when a member of the parliament demanded to know what you intend to do to provide relief to our tribal brethren peoples, you did not reply a single word. Still, in those times when the Karelian and Ingrian issues formed a part of our foreign policy, you at least tried to do what you could, most recently in Geneva in 1921-22. We consider it our right to expect more from you than from, for example, your predecessor. You and the cabinet you are a member of bear a heavy responsibility here, one which will not allow you to do nothing, even if due to some diplomatic considerations you are unable to make any official statements regarding the matter. Those who hold the Karelian and Ingrian cause dear have been accused of anti-Russian sentiments — not by the Soviets themselves, but by our own leftists. These accusations against the Soviet Union are completely baseless because it is absolutely obvious that we must avoid conflicts with them, given the present state of our armed forces. I am quite convinced that our leftist, and sadly also our centrist, press have provoked the Soviet political class to anti-Finnish sentiment.

These papers have made fictitious claims regarding our intentions and amplified any politically meaningless statements that they can into scenarios of horror. For example, they claim we have discussed moving the Russo-Finnish border to the Urals, which we have never written or spoken about. The statements made by the president Bushujeff of Eastern Karelia about a year ago must have been provoked by the press as well. He claimed that the Finns dream of moving the border to the river Yenisei.

But the most preposterous provocation our country's press has been guilty of during our independence was carried out by *Svenska Pressen*[74] and *Sosiaalidemokraatti*,[75] when they pretended the pamphlet "Herää Suomi!" (Awaken Finland), published in 1923, was actually a recent AKS publication. This publication, which is over 13 years old, produced by the veterans of the Karelian uprising, was unscrupulously distorted into a compromising, damaging document, parts of which the Izvestia published with delight on May 14, 1936.

Is this the correct procedure for the press toward their country? Not only the Izvestia but also the rest of the Soviet press milked this material for a long time in a campaign of vile attacks against our country. It must be asked: has the government paid enough attention to this type of behavior, which quite clearly is harmful to our country? It is obvious that both our red and yellow press are to blame at least in part for the arrogant attack on Finland by the leader of the St. Petersburg chapter of the communist party. So much has been said about the danger of internal fascism that it supposedly allows Zhdanov[76] cause to believe that Finland is prepared to allow the fascist states to use our country as a base for an attack against Soviet Russia. We have the right to demand that the government respond directly to these Russian provocations and insults.

The meek and servile actions of our most recent cabinets seem to have placed our entire people under a strange inferiority complex so that one has had many times to ask if this people can still think of their nation as a sovereign state. This is not evident only in our attitude toward the Soviet Union, but also toward Scandinavia. It is true, that the parliamentary group I am a member of was initially prepared to accept our embracing of Scandinavia in our foreign policy, but only in a manner that does not violate our sovereignty and our national honor. I have read

---

[74] *The Swedish Press*, a Swedish language tabloid published in Helsinki. It ceased publication in 1974.
[75] *Finland's Social Democrat* is the party paper of the Social Democrat party. It is still being published under the title *Demokraatti (The Democrat)*.
[76] Andrei Zhdanov (1896-1948) was a Soviet political ideologist.

many statements in the Swedish-speaking press that the Finnish people have no right to advance any Finnish nationalist goals, not regarding the Finnish university nor a Finnish culture after this agreement. Supposedly this can damage our relationship with Scandinavia. This weakness in our nationalist feeling is apparent also in the way our left-wing press — instead of accusing Russia of violations in Karelia and Ingria — point their fingers at the nationalists here, for whom the question of tribal unity is sacred and who ask for nothing but for the Soviets to keep their own side of the international agreements they have entered into. At a time like this, when the geopolitical crisis approaches a boiling point and Finland is in a vulnerable position between an aggressive, expansionist, militarily-mighty Soviet Union, and the Scandinavian nations — who in reality would form a military vacuum behind us, were the moment of truth to arrive — we must ask our government to pursue a policy that takes the requirements of our national honor into account. For a nation that forgoes honor has no respect from other nations, nor sympathy from the great powers which are now deciding the fate of the world. For the same reason, we demand our government act to assist our tribal brother peoples, which is a demand we make not only for the sake of our national honor but for the sake of human and divine righteousness.

The Path of Self Denial

AKS Oath Ceremony, December 6, 1936

Independence Day, which we celebrate today, is a day of great memories. But at the same time, it should be a day for great plans for the future. To those of you who intend to vow loyalty to the most holy symbol of our society, the black flag of the AKS, and to the ideals it represents, it is a day of great *promises*.

The promise you are about to give is strict and demanding if given with a sincere mind and if given not primarily in speech, but also from your heart. You make a promise of sacrifice; you promise to devote yourself and your industry, that is, all of yourself, to our Fatherland. If you make this promise in the sincere and honest manner of a Finn, thereafter in many ways your hands will be tied and your life will no longer be exclusively your own. If you are truly Finns — as we believe you to be — you will remain faithful to your oath, so faithful to the point of being prepared to stand and fall by it. If you take the oath to give yourself over to the Fatherland, it means that you will willingly carry the cross pressing down on our entire people. It means both rejoicing and lamenting together with the people. It means self-discipline, self-denial; it means walking a path on which you will encounter difficulties, sorrow, and perhaps the worst of all, even shame.

We have the hope that the things I mention are dear to you because you have come here. Since after all, you have seen that the path of the citizen devoted to the Fatherland is a way without external honor, without material benefit. You have seen and heard how our association has been slandered and degraded. So why have you come here, if not to partake in our degradation? That is our faith, the only thing that gives us the strength to hope, believe, and suffer for the greatness of the Fatherland.

And yet, all of our labor and struggle will be in vain, if He, whose breath can blow away entire nations into the dust of history, and before whom every human being must bend their knee, opposes us: Lord God. Today we have a special reason to bow our heads before him, humble in prayer, and hope that he will not abandon us as he has did not abandon our forefathers, nor us until now.

It is through God's abundant mercy that we have come this far, achieved what little we have. It is with him that this people have risen from blood and ashes; even when its path had appeared to reach its end, they have endured cold and starvation. It is in Him, the righteous God of our forefathers, that we must take refuge in today and pray to. Pray that He may, in the name of everything He did for them, allow our love and faith to remain strong. God himself, our refuge and our fortress, will keep us safe in the storms we see gathering in horizons now. And keep us humble through it.

The Danger from the Sky

Two Parliamentary Remarks

I. December 17, 1936

The parliamentary group of the IKL has proposed an additional 90,000,000 marks to strengthen our anti-aircraft artillery. This has been denied by the ministry of finance for monetary reasons. Our proposal would mean speeding the basic program of acquisitions for the armed forces faster than has been planned. Many have suggested in the press recently that the need to expedite arming our troops is becoming urgent, even centrists. They have suggested issuing government bonds to fund this military spending.

The geopolitical situation is extremely tense at the moment. A global conflagration that may swallow our small country for simple reasons of geography may ignite at any moment. We also must take into account the process of armament taking place across the border. It is a matter of public record that the Soviet congress of Moscow has decided to create the greatest military machine the world has ever seen. The plan is to, for example, double the peacetime strength of the Red Army to three million men. They will increase their air force threefold and train 50,000 new pilots. This is a frightening situation, which should cause our small country to make every effort to ensure the technical capability of our defense forces. Our starting point must always be that even a small country should equip itself so that a superpower may decide that it is not worth the trouble to invade them. We can also point to reverse examples where a nation that has become a power vacuum has attracted attention from the great powers and tempted them with desires of conquest. Given the current geopolitical situation and the arms race it has created, it seems that the schedule for these military acquisitions, which would take 6 years to complete, is hopelessly slow. It is hopelessly slow for the simple reason that in part, some of the armaments acquired will become obsolete in that time. But of course most importantly, because our military may reach their full capability far too late. The IKL has seen it necessary to propose further developing our anti-aircraft capability, fully in the knowledge that it is presently at such a primitive level that we are practically defenseless. We also recognize that the program of basic armaments is itself inadequate because even if it were to be implemented 100%, our defenses would still be inadequate. This is not warmongering; we simply wish to provide our people with the means to carry out their most basic duty, which is self-defense. This is a case of genuine peacemaking because it is aimed at protecting primarily our nation's civilians.

A foreign power's airplanes—albeit "ghost" planes—are already buzzing overhead. It is amazing how frivolous the attitude of the Parliament has been toward this matter. The proposal of placing a functionary responsible for civilian defense in the ministry of interior, and thus meeting the most primitive requirements of modern national defense, was rejected on the basis that the task of defending civilians belongs to the armed forces, not the ministry of interior. But seeing as how the military lacks the funds, it was most frivolous to block this project, which in reality should be expanded to cover the entire populace and which indeed would have been the task of this functionary.

As an example of the attitude taken by nations who have a desire to defend themselves toward civilian defense and antiaircraft artillery, I will mention a few facts regarding the work of the Soviet Union's voluntary air defense association, Osoaviakhim. It was founded in 1923, at which point it was immediately joined by three million citizens. By 1935 membership had grown to 14 million. The purpose of this association is to organize all the Soviet people to deter the danger from the air, should war break out. For this purpose, even children have been equipped with gas masks and given training on using them. Another remarkable fact about this association is how many women are involved in it. 1,300,000 of their female members have received a medal for their work for the association. An example of their vigor is their plan to train one million workers for the defense of Leningrad alone by the end of the year 1936. They train not only engineers and administrative staff, but also residential building superintendents, teachers, warehouse managers, even nursery teachers.

Against this background, our own people's indifference toward matters of life and death seems preposterous. Most of the responsibility falls on Parliament, who have, as I already pointed out, rejected even modest proposals to rectify this matter, on very lightweight grounds. As for the social democrats, you would think they would want to follow the example of a country with a Marxist system in matters of national self-defense and in maintaining a will to do so among the population. Our neighbor to the east has focused on developing their air force and has made frightening breakthroughs. Their bombers can reach high speeds, and they are capable of carrying thousands of kilograms of explosive, incendiary, and gas bombs. Still, it is by no means hopeless to attempt to defend ourselves against this threat, if our army and our anti-aircraft artillery are updated to efficient modern standards.

We must remember that modern warfare is devastating, and it targets above all the defenseless civilian population, including women and children. When we speak of air defense, it is defending this unarmed civilian population from this carnage. One would wish that we would have at least this much unanimity, for how else can we stand before the future generations, that is, if such future generations are ever born in this country. The government must also find the necessary funds to carry out this essential work and to find the courage to tell the truth to the populace so that they do not wake up to their homes and towns going up in flames. The IKL proposes we fortify air defenses in any way possible. We should use the monies we have suggested on planes, anti-aircraft artillery, and machine guns, as well as civilian defense, which is an integral and very efficient part of air defense. If we plan adequately for this, even our small nation can stop the enemy from the air, no matter how dangerous the enemy may be. Our only option is to defend ourselves. It is up to us whether we do it well or badly.

II. November 29, 1937

The parliamentary group of the IKL has proposed an additional 90,000,000 marks to strengthen our aerial defense. This has been denied by the ministry of finance, "because the defense force's basic acquisitions program is being handled by a special committee, and because making proposals of this type should be done by the government," as the ministry states. When we were deliberating a similar proposal from our group for our last national budget, it was denied for monetary reasons. If rejecting a proposal for defending our civilians based on financial reasons — in times of economic upturn, no less — is justified, then the rationalizations presented this time in support of rejection are completely invalid as well. After all, we have read in the papers that the committee deliberated that the budget must be raised. The prices of military material have risen so quickly, that the annual budget barely covers the originally planned acquisitions. In geopolitically difficult times such as these, we cannot possibly wait for years for all the needed equipment to arrive for our military. It is downright frightening to see how slow the parliamentary process has been, even for the committee created specifically for this purpose. And the parliament rejects all the proposals for improving our military, even the most essential ones, on the pretext that there already is a committee working on these matters. There have been attempts to excuse rejecting our proposals on the basis that the 1938 budget increases spending on our air force. This is false because the rising prices mean that things do not improve, rather they barely stay as they are.

It is true, as the minister of defense mentioned during a certain other deliberation, that we must maintain absolute neutrality. But it is also true, and this also was mentioned by the minister as well, that there are some irresponsible elements in our nation that seek to break said neutrality. I take it that the irresponsible elements he refers to are those who have begun, as the Moscow VII communist congress dictated, to form "people's fronts," also here in our country. Even if our goal is complete neutrality, it seems unlikely that it will be possible, due to our geopolitically dangerous position. Should the Soviet Union enter into a military conflict with some major power, they will try to protect their trade routes to and from St. Petersburg, while their enemy will of course try to sever them. Large military operations on the Baltic can hardly be expected to function without violating our national sovereignty. In case of war, the Soviet Union would probably try to use our harbors, rather than those of other countries in the Baltic. Above all, we should remember that Åland, if taken over by a large power capable of fortifying it, would mean absolute domination over the Baltic for that nation. It forms the most dangerous military power vacuum within our sphere, and it is relentlessly being watched by the Soviets. These are merely a few examples of how quickly we may lose our neutrality in the case of a major European war.

I should like to reiterate again that our parliamentary group's proposal is meant to protect the civilian population in times of war. We must remember that modern warfare is not an army fighting against another army, but nation against nation, a people against another people. It is a war of extermination, in which each belligerent tries to eliminate the vital, central, societal hubs, mainly large cities. In wars of extermination such as these, the main casualties are the unarmed civilians, typically attacked from the air with bombing raids, which try to crush the population's spirit. Recent examples are wars such as the one in Abyssinia, the civil war in Spain, and especially the war between China and Japan, in which there have been more civilian than military casualties. It is perfectly obvious that our country is extremely vulnerable in this regard. There is not a single city or town that the Soviet bombers cannot reach within two hours of war being declared. There are more Soviet air forces in the St. Petersburg area now than we can deploy even in times of war. The 18 military airfields of the St. Petersburg area are situated so that only 4 of them are designed for attacks against Estonia. Eight of them are further north than Kuopio. All of these airfields have an attack range that extends further west than Finland. And let us not forget the so-called "ghost flights" that have been reported in northern Finland. They may be connected to military preparations we know nothing about. The fact that our government refuses to even acknowledge their existence does not make them any less real. The Swedish military does admit that they take place. We must also remember how Russian planes cross the border at the Karelian Isthmus and how modern equipment permits photography from a distance of up to three kilometers. The Soviet Union is especially fond of building enormous bomber planes. Their only mission is to destroy means of production, roads, warehouses, and population centers far behind enemy lines. They are purely offensive weapons. They have also experimented with transporting large groups of airborne saboteurs, that is invading paratroopers, with large planes. In the sparsely populated areas of northern Finland — especially aided by our domestic communists, who may be capable of great sabotage and disorder — such troops may have significant capabilities.

It is obvious that we will never be able to compete with the Soviet Union in this type of arms race, but that is not the issue here anyway. It is a matter of each nation and each individual's most basic duty — the duty of self-defense. We must raise our capabilities to such a level that the Soviet Union understands that it is not to their benefit to try to violate our national sovereignty. As I said, clearly we have no means of acquiring as many planes as could match whatever the Soviets may send our way. But we must have enough to defend our residential and industrial centers and so our army can coordinate aerial reconnaissance and battle missions. At present our air force is insufficient, but certainly, with improvements and reorganization, we can easily reach that level.

I have heard it said that at the moment it is difficult to find anti-aircraft artillery anywhere even if one is willing to pay for it, but even so, we must acquire more fighter planes, they being the most effective form of combating bombers, in the final analysis. Some say that our defense budget is too large as it is. If we compare it with the defense budgets of countries with geopolitically far less endangered positions, the findings are surprising. An official German publication, "Rüstung der Welt" finds — these figures are from 1935 — that our per capita military spending is less than that of, for example, Denmark, a country that has been called positively nihilistic when it comes to national defense. According to these statistics, only Norway spends less on national defense among the European countries than we do. Based on a statistic from 1936, all our military expenses were 209 marks and 80 pfenning per citizen. In Sweden, a country ruled by Social Democrats, the same expenses were 286.14 marks, which is significantly more, not to speak of the Soviet Union, which spend 3523.81 marks per citizen. Finland is the only nation in the world that continues to pay its foreign debts at the moment but feels it can afford to neglect its national defense. Besides our weak air force, we should also look at other significant shortages in our armed forces. Our infantry lacks sufficient firearms, not to speak of our anti-tank weaponry, artillery, armored vehicles, etc. But given the confidential nature of such matters, I will not bring them up in detail here.

We are next-door neighbors of the world's most militaristic nation, which has harnessed their entire state, economy, and population for one single purpose: war. They have the most advanced air force and gas weaponry in the world, and recently military experts have discovered that they also have the world's most efficient fleet of submarines. The fleet is enormous in the Gulf of Finland also, where our most strategic islands have been demilitarized based on the Tarto treaty. In these times we cannot delay equipping our military, and especially air defense, any longer.

It has been said that an air force is the most effective protection for a poor nation. If we cannot convince you of the need for this, then perhaps the sight of enemy planes within our national borders can. This is a problem our foreign policy has been unable to solve. Our nation's economy is also especially healthy, so no one can say that this is economically unfeasible. Releasing government bonds for this purpose would also get the job done quickly, even though I do not even consider it necessary at this moment. We can afford to reinforce our air defense directly from our national budget. How will our current generation, living in an economic upturn, and the politicians they have elected to represent them, avoid being condemned by history, if they leave our country and people defenseless, facing destruction?

The Battle Against Bolshevism

Two Parliamentary Remarks

I. April 13, 1937

Our present government has shown an unusual degree of interest in protecting the national sovereignty of Spain. We are now deliberating on a law, which, if passed, would allow for the incarceration of those who recruit volunteers for Spain for a year, and the volunteers themselves for six months.

However, clearly, there are important matters of national sovereignty closer to us than that of Spain. In a situation when we cannot even protect our own borders against violations, it is ridiculous to give millions to secure Spain's borders. It is pathetic that Finland, unable to project its own maritime borders and keep Soviet agents from confiscating the catch from Finnish fishermen, sometimes from within our waters, sends Finnish captains and admirals to protect Spain's national maritime borders. Would not these said admirals and captains be desperately needed on our own waters, judging from the gross violations that already have happened?

However, it is incredibly difficult to successfully gain additional funding for a purpose such as this. It seems that Spain's national borders and national interests are closer to the heart of this parliament than those of Finland. Our foreign policy seems entirely based on advancing the interests of the pro-Soviet block. We can be sure that the Soviet Union will make sure that the exportation of weapons and ammunition to Spain will not be interrupted because of this policy of non-intervention.

Now that the Soviet Union coerced the League of Nations into accepting trade sanctions against Italy, it still did not prevent them from selling massive amounts of gasoline and lubricants to the Italian military, a trade which earned the Soviets fortunes. Finland was forced to retract the sanctions along with the other member states of the League of Nations. I am convinced that Finland, whose main priority seems to be to prevent volunteers from joining Franco's army and whose Parliament tolerates the most shameless slander toward Franco's liberation movement, will nevertheless soon enough send their own representative to the French government. For nothing can now prevent it: the Soviet attempt to create a Bolshevik state in the Mediterranean will be crushed. If it were not so, we would be yet another step closer to the Downfall of the West, predicted by respected philosopher Spengler, the downfall which has thus been prevented only by the iron resistance of the fascist states. The Non-Intervention Committee can, however, delay the only reasonable and just outcome in Spain. After all, at a meeting of the Committee in London, on March 24, 1937, the German ambassador von Ribbentrop protested that the Non-Intervention Committee had "been used for propaganda purposes."

Such propaganda was repeated, on behalf of the Red Spanish government, here in this Parliament on March the 23rd by Cay Sundström.[77] It would be most urgent to take steps regarding his speech, if not for the fact that he is not taken seriously even among his own party. It is impossible for MP Sundström to seriously claim, that the Soviet Union has not supported the red government of Spain. Without such support, it would have been impossible for it to last for as long as it has. According to statistics, the Soviet Union has shipped enormous quantities of military materials to Spain. Apparently, the Soviets have provided the Spanish Bolsheviks with 200 fighter planes, over 200 tanks, machine guns, rifles, ammunition, and other similar materials. Some troops have technical assistance from Soviet-Russian staff.

---

[77] Cay Sundström (1902-1959) was a social democrat MP.

Others are made up of purely Russian infantry. Against this background, it is poisonously ironic to say something like Cay Sundström said: "There is no battle against religion, since after all the majority of the supporters of the legal government are religious." This "religious" army has destroyed hundreds of Spain's churches and monasteries, murdered and tortured hundreds of priests, nuns, and monks. It must be said that the religious sentiments of this mob are rather unusual. Perhaps they share the same religion with MP Sundström, since his remarks show that this Parliament has been infiltrated by propagandists whose worldviews are utterly corrupted by communism.

Italy let it be known that they will not permit a Bolshevik state to be formed at the mouth of the Mediterranean. It should obviously be in the interests of all of Europe to prevent this threat. We must therefore fight any attempt to weaken, even indirectly, the fight against Bolshevism in Spain. The national army in Spain combats it just like the Finnish army did in 1918. We all know the bitterness toward the Swedish government, which refused to allow the transport of arms through their territory, even though the White Finnish Army fought the Bolsheviks not only for our own Fatherland but for Scandinavia and the rest of Europe. Sweden's red government also tried to prevent volunteers from traveling to Finland, and those few who did make the trip received barbaric treatment upon their return home to Sweden. Although the mater of Sweden is farther from us than Sweden was in 1918, certain comparisons can still be made. The law proposed by the government, which would imprison volunteers who depart for Spain would target only those volunteers who wish to fight on Franco's side. Apparently, no one has wished to go to Spain to fight for the Bolsheviks, but if someone did, it would surely be no loss for our country to be rid of such scum.

Speaking of recruiting volunteers, this has not been done in Finland, and it does not seem realistic that it could be done in the future. The law is unnecessary in this regard. It is my own opinion that we should remain officially neutral in these matters. And we have the red peril threatening our own borders as well, even within them, and we must save young Finnish blood for this. However, having said so, I do not see it as fulfilling the requirements of honor that we should prevent Finnish lads who wish to battle Bolshevism wherever the opportunity to do so may arise. Let us remind ourselves that we have had in this country men such as Myhrberg,[78] who have fought for the freedom of lands just as distant as Spain, whose memory is now respected by the people. We must salute the men who are prepared to defend the freedom of Spain and Europe against the Asian hordes, not threaten them with imprisonment.

II. April 5, 1938

Looking at the government's proposed additions to the 1938 national budget, one notices that odd item of 1,630,000 marks for sovereignty monitoring on Spanish borders. At the same time, the government allots 1,586,000 marks to safeguard our defenses on our eastern border. It must be asked if a small country like Finland really has millions to squander on protecting the borders of distant Spain, especially when the defenses on our eastern border have significant deficiencies, ones that would require much more than a million and a half to repair. Or does the government feel like this allotted sum is enough to deter the constant and ever more outrageous border violations to our east and southeast? Is it not necessary to increase the strength of our anti-aircraft artillery at the border, to stop the so-called ghost flights, whose real purpose is to photograph the terrain for the Soviet army's terrain orientation? This is an expense far greater than the 812,000 marks now proposed by the government since that is barely enough for one proper anti-aircraft cannon. Additionally, the government should absolutely have allotted additional monies to add to our

---

[78] August Myhrberg, (1797 -1867) was Swedish-Finnish officer who took part in several popular uprisings and wars in Europe.

border guards' strength. As for the money to be sent to Spain, it is only a little over a year, that we already spent 1,700,000 marks for this purpose. Now we are to spend an additional 1,630,000 marks, that is, 44,000 more than we are to spend on our own national defense at our eastern border.

When we cannot guarantee the sovereignty of our own borders, how can we afford to squander our money on defending the borders of a country as distant as Spain? It can be said that as a member of the League of Nations we are bound by international treaties. This is certainly true. But it is my opinion that we should leave these treaties and actually the League itself, since it has turned out to be an interest group for a few superpowers. We can certainly accept the law on non-intervention, but under no circumstances should a small country such as Finland spend its own money for this purpose.

As for the border itself, defending it has turned out to be an absolute joke. French military materials pour into red Spain, as well as troops to the "Brigada Internationale," which is a shock troop of the global revolution and carries the Comintern badges. Is this non-intervention at the French border, where there are Finnish guards as well, now that the reds in Spain suffer catastrophic defeats, supposed to re-organize in France and then return to Catalonia? As for the Soviet Union's respect for these laws, we all know it already. After all the Soviets have sent masses of war material to Spain, without which the red Spanish army would have been utterly shattered a long time ago. And there are also tens of thousands of Soviet Russians fighting for the red Spanish cause.

On the opposite side, Germany and especially Italy have also interfered significantly in the Spanish Civil War. It is due primarily to these two nations, Germany and Italy, that we do not now have a Bolshevik barbarian state in the Iberian Peninsula, which allied with the Soviet Union could possibly spell the downfall of the entire Western Civilization. It is due only to divine grace that Finland is free of the danger that currently threatens

Spain, and therefore we do not have the right to delay the victory of the nationalists in Spain by allowing this expenditure.

Finland's Foreign Policy

Parliamentary Remarks, November 23, 1937

In these geopolitically unstable times, the government's foreign policies have attracted an unusual interest both in cabinet parties and in the opposition. Our foreign policy has, during both our present foreign minister as well as his predecessor, been focused on maintaining good relations with all our neighboring states. As such there is nothing wrong with that, and neither is there anything wrong with wanting to keep out of the sphere of influence of any major powers.

However, these ideals are pursued by our current foreign minister in a manner that is not altogether convincing of perfectly sincere desires of absolute neutrality. Specifically, his excellency the foreign minister has pursued our policies when it comes to Russia in a manner that has resulted in a loss of respect for our country, both in the Soviet Union as well as in the eyes of many other powerful states. It was noted especially in Germany and Italy that the minister made his first foreign trip in office to Moscow. In general, the minister has clearly focused on a pro-Soviet approach in everything. To the extent that has been necessary to make it known in Germany, via unofficial channels, we are in fact not a part of a Soviet power block.

Regarding our government's policies toward the Soviet Union, it is impossible not to note that the more accepting our government becomes toward the insults that come from that direction, the more daring and outrageous these insults and attacks become. It already has been said here that a certain well-known person has noted that The Soviet Union tried to directly control Finland's government. Despite this, it cannot be said that our relations with the Soviet Union have improved. This has been a matter of great difficulty for the government. I would like to say that the only way to gain the respect of greater powers is by firm and determined policies. I refuse to believe that our relations can be improved, for example, with the 100,000 marks our Parliament recently allocated for the opening ceremony of the Moscow embassy, at a time when the border violations and the exiles of our Ingrian tribal brethren continue. When it comes to aerial border violations, which have been noted internationally, it is now time to demand a straight answer from the cabinet: has the Soviet Union answered the political note sent to them by the government?

It is a common claim that an answer was given, but the government's answers have been evasive. But still I ask: what does the government intend to do to stop these violations? Can there really be no anti-aircraft artillery at the Karelian Isthmus fortifications, or have they been ordered not to act? It is my understanding that Finland stands to lose the remaining vestiges of our respect in the international arena, if we cannot defend our borders. I suppose that the discussions in which foreign minister Holsti[79] engaged in Moscow referred also to easing the position of fishers in the Gulf of Finland. The actual achievements in this matter speak for themselves: our fishermen have had their catch robbed even in our own national waters, and they find their nets routinely destroyed by Russian ships.

I also suppose that his excellency the foreign minister has negotiated with commissar Litvinov to put an end to the mass deportations. But after his visit to Moscow, they have begun again, in almost all Ingrian villages, in northern, central, and southern Ingria. It is estimated that after the minister's visit, 3,000 Ingrians have been deported to Siberia and elsewhere in Russia. From the Kelto municipality alone, the GPU[80] has abducted 500

---

[79] The minister referred to here is Rudolf Holsti (1881-1945), who was Finland's foreign minister 1919-1922 and 1937-1938.
[80] GPU: Gosudarstvennoe politicheskoe upravlenie "State Political Administration," the intelligence service of the Soviet Union.

men. In the parishes of Vuolle, Miikkulainen, Lempäälä, and Valkeasaari many villages are utterly empty by now. In Kelto, Rääpyvä, and Toksova preparations for the same are underway. We really should not be cozying up to the USSR and spending thousands of marks to host a party for our new embassy in Moscow.

Much has been said about the League of Nations here. In my opinion, we should begin to seriously consider whether we still have reason to continue being one of its member states. The politics in the League should be neutral, but they certainly have not been since the Soviet Union was accepted as a member. The Soviets wield significant influence, to the point that the League can now be said to be an extension of it, one that is in constant conflict with the nations that form the anti-Soviet front. The legitimacy of the League has been a topic of discussion even in those countries that typically have been among its greatest supporters. For example, in the Swedish press, there has been great concern that neutrality, which is of great importance in the Nordic countries and other small nations as well, is contrary to the League's regulations regarding sanctions. As the *Dagens Nyheter*[81] journalist points out, if Sweden were to be invited to join the League in 1920, and it had been then as it is now, with the present catastrophic state of affairs, no one in Swedish society would have supported joining. The paper goes on to say, "This would have been considered an ill-considered adventure, incompatible with even the most primitive sense of concern for the peace and security of our nation."

Similar voices are heard in our domestic press as well, even the centrist ones, not to mention the right-wing ones. Even the social democrats have made similar remarks. *Helsingin Sanomat*[82] says, "It seems that the League cannot be anything but a political discussion club." Everyone is familiar with the speech of the Swedish foreign minister Sandler, in which he discussed what

---

[81] *Daily News* is a Swedish newspaper. It is still published today.
[82] *Helsinki Times* is Finland's largest newspaper, still published today.

security guarantees the League offers to small nations. He clearly believes that Sweden must have the daring to advance their own interests, independently of the League if necessary.

We must begin the earnest discussion about leaving the League here in Finland also. But it seems it is out of the question with our present foreign minister, who is a true admirer of the League. And if I understand this correctly, he is also the chairman of the League's committee on disarmament. And if ever when discussing budget it is appropriate to care about squandered money, it is now that we consider the millions that have been used to represent us in the League. Our cabinet seems positively ridiculous when donating curtains for the meeting hall of the League and has our foreign minister donating them ceremonially.

If there is one thing that our foreign minister must be harshly criticized for, it is for voting in favor of red Spain re-joining the League of Nations. This action is nothing short of a mockery of the ideals that prevented a wave of anarchy from washing over our country, the same wave that now washes over Spain, courtesy of the so-called Valencia government. It is true that pro-Soviet propaganda has spread all over the world in favor of Red Spain, and yet no one can deny the truth of minister Goebbels' statement, that the war in Spain is the Comintern's show of strength before a global takeover. This fact is also recognized in the Anglo-Saxon nations. And if we look at the rage that Soviet Spain has directed toward the Church, one can only find similarities in the fate of the martyr church of the Soviet Union. On February 2 of last year, 16,000 priests or monks and 11 bishops have been murdered.

In some parishes, in the red areas, the percentage of the clergy that has been murdered is 40% and in many cases as high as 80%. Of the 2,200 consecrated buildings in Madrid, none remain open, and most have been destroyed. Of the 1,778 places of worship in Barcelona, only the cathedral remains intact. The party secretary for the Spanish communists, Jose Diaz, confirmed as much in a speech he delivered last May 5: "In the regions under our control, no churches remain." Looking at these numbers it is impossible not to agree with the Englishman Arthur Bryant, who states in the *Observer*: "Red Spain is not a constitutional republic, is it an inferno."

It is a dictatorship of this sort to which our foreign minister gave his support, a dictatorship that has as its stated objective the destruction of religion and all of Western Civilization from the Iberian Peninsula, replacing it with Asian barbarism. It was entirely correct when the *Daily Mail* remarked on the failure of Red Spain in the League of Nations as follows:

> *Blocking Bolshevik Spain from the League of Nations is the best thing that has happened during these parliamentary sessions. Soviet Spain only has the support of one-third of the nation's population. The ruling committee of Valencia, which is guilty of innumerable murders and other crimes, has lost the privilege of sitting at a table with civilized nations. The League, which the Bolsheviks have so often abused in order to spread propaganda of the most pernicious sort, has for once displayed wisdom in removing the Spanish robbers.*

The Spanish question has been dealt with here in Parliament twice before. First, we dealt with the so-called non-intervention millions for the second time when the Parliament passed a law penalizing any volunteers who wish to travel to Spain to take part in the conflict. The previous time, our parliamentary group stated that our policy regarding Spain will become a fiasco because sooner or later we must recognize the legitimacy of the Franco government. And that time will come soon. For example, such a supporter of Red Spain as Leon Blum has lost all hope regarding the victory of the reds, as evidenced by the speech he gave at a meeting of the French parliament's socialists. The flexible politics of England are the first to reflect this fact. Their foreign minister recently gave a speech commending Franco, and their government has already established a diplomatic relationship with general Franco's government. It seems certain that they will recall their ambassador from Red Spain. Without a doubt, Finland's government too must eventually accept and recognize Franco's government. The only lamentable details here are the actions of our foreign minister in the League, which can only be described as scandalous. I know that the minister has done what he could in the League to advance, for example, the Karelian issue. Because of this, I wish I did not have to speak as harshly as I now must: grave errors have been committed in Finland's foreign policy during our independence but never errors as great as have been committed by our present foreign minister — with the exception of Mr. Holsti's previous time as foreign minister.

Artur Sirk[83]: In Memoriam

Artur Sirk's Funeral, Helsinki Old Church, October 9, 1937

Grace and peace be yours in abundance through the knowledge of God and of Jesus our Lord. Amen. Jesus says: "I am the resurrection and the life. The one who believes in me will live, even though they die."

Dear friends: we have gathered around the casket of a great freedom fighter. Artur Sirk, whose memory we are here to give our respects and whom we shall now lie to rest, was, if anyone, a fighter from his earliest youth. He was a fighter as a youth, who fought for the freedom of Estonia, as a leader of Estonia's freedom movement. However, the most grueling battles he had to fight most recently, as he was imprisoned and hounded from one country to another as a hunted animal.

It is not the place of a minister who stands at a gravesite to review the political achievements of the deceased, even in the case of such a politically significant person as Artur Sirk. But I believe it is my duty, as a servant of the Lord, to let it be known that Artur Sirk's motives were pure and unselfish and that the cause he fought for was true and noble. This is a truth we must dare to speak out loud as we lay this fighter to rest.

When thinking of Artur Sirk's tragic fate, we find ourselves asking: "Why must his life end this way?" We come to the eternal problem of suffering, which makes any imperfect creature become mute with awe, at the face of eternity. There is nothing

---

[83] Judge Artur Sirk, the young and brilliant leader of the Estonian freedom movement, was forced to spend the last years of his life in exile, in England, the Netherlands, and Luxembourg due to persecution by agents of his country's rulers. This persecution ended in Judge Sirk's violent death in the town of Echternach, Luxembourg. His Finnish friends had his body transported to Finland, and he is now buried in the Hietaniemi cemetery in Helsinki.

else to say than say, as David did: "I was silent; I would not open my mouth, for you are the one who has done this."

One thing is certain: God had special plans for him. This lone fighter had to call for the Lord from the depths of his soul. I have here, in my hand, Artur Sirk's own personal Bible. He has bookmarked Psalm 140. It seems that in his final days, he had turned to the Lord with this prayer. I shall read from it, in his own native language:

> *Rescue me, Lord, from evildoers; protect me from the violent, who devise evil plans in their hearts and stir up war every day. They make their tongues as sharp as a serpent's; the poison of vipers is on their lips. Keep me safe, Lord, from the hands of the wicked; protect me from the violent, who devise ways to trip my feet. The arrogant have hidden a snare for me; they have spread out the cords of their net and have set traps for me along my path. I say to the Lord, "You are my God." Hear, Lord, my cry for mercy. Sovereign Lord, my strong deliverer, you shield my head in the day of battle. Do not grant the wicked their desires, Lord; do not let their plans succeed.*

(Ps. 140: 1-8.)

We ask ourselves, "Why does it seem, from a human perspective that the Lord, whom this man turned to in distress, did not seem to hear him?" We must remember that the Lord has designs for entire nations, not merely individuals. No movement for national awakening has advanced without sacrifice. Many an individual has been recognized by their people as a true leader, only after they have been crowned by a martyr's crown of thorns. We must believe that the fight for justice and truth was not dashed on the paving stones of a street in Echternach. We must believe that through the sacrifice of individuals, God allows righteous causes to triumph.

Great as the work for nationalist resurrection may be, we still must remember that even such movements are finite. They will eventually be extinguished in the night of time. But there shall be a resurrection that calls each individual and each nation to the throne of God. This is the resurrection that the quote "I am the resurrection and the life" refers to. Then, all tombstones will fall to the side and everyone must face eternal judgment. Those with good deeds will step into the resurrection of life, which those whose deeds have been evil will enter the resurrection of damnation. Then this particular deceased person, just as all of his opponents and enemies, will receive justice that cannot be corrupted or intimidated. This judgment comes from no human court but rather, righteousness itself.

We hope that this fighter, who had to call for God's mercy in a distant land, far from his family, his own people and his friends, has found his way to God and is at rest. It is in a moment of heavy grief such as this, full of death and dissipation, that we recall the words of Jesus, which are the only true consolation for you, the grieving widow and the daughter of this fallen hero, and to us, his friends on both sides of the Gulf of Finland: "I am the resurrection and the life. The one who believes in me will live, even though they die."

We Hear the Next War Approaching

AKS Anniversary to Army Officers, February 22, 1938

As the spring approaches, so does the 20th anniversary of an independent Finland's defense force. When the leader of the AKS ordered me to give this speech to our army, I immediately thought of the curious coincidence that it is today, 20 years to the day, that those troops I belonged to departed for the south, having first liberated the cities and towns of Ostrobothnia. Therefore I, too, had the opportunity to give my own microscopic contribution to our Fatherland's liberation. In these depressing times, one's mind often wanders to those days. No one who was not there can imagine the spirit of the army of the freedom war. Who could forget those trains packed with lads, as they traveled south! They carried youth and idealism that was rewarded with suffering and death. They were untrained, badly armed, and starving, and yet this army carried out the mightiest feat in all the history of Finland. And some of them went on to spill their blood on the battlefields of Estonia, Karelia, and Ingria.

When addressing today's military, I ask myself, are they still inspired by the spirit of the freedom war, which could work miracles? This spirit is no longer there in those veteran associations, who claim that political organizations should not be allowed to honor the monuments to the heroic dead. They may have had their time of inspiration, but it has been extinguished by these dark times. They have not seen through the darkness that there still are youth who — to use an often mocked phrase — dares to dream. If only this youth were never to grow so old, that they are content to be nothing but a lackey for the system!

Although it would be unreasonable to expect the kind of

daring we have seen in war from the military in these times of peace, it is still extraordinary how hard our officers have worked to create an army for our nation, practically out of nothing. Badly paid, misunderstood, often even despised, these men have carried out their essential work in these years of independence. Without complaint, they have served the republic and the government, regardless of the colors it happens to follow. Accuse them of anything else, but never question their loyalty to our country! But they can do no more than their own duty.

It has only been in recent years that we have become aware of severe shortcomings in their equipment. It is only recently that the Parliament was made aware that if war were to break out, we would have to send our best youth unarmed against the enemy. One imagines that this fact will burn the hearts of any true military leader, one who works with conscripts. The ineptitude and slowness in amending these problems must be a heavy burden. Why does the committee suggest carrying out the required acquisitions over many years, when he already hears the next war approaching? What horrors must we witness for the gears of parliamentarism to begin to turn?

Finland's military expenditures are smaller than those of any other European country, except for Denmark, although our geopolitical position is among the most dangerous on the globe. In the meantime, Switzerland updated its military in one year by taking a 3 billion mark loan. Germany built their army in three months, so that Hitler, the leader of the German people, can say with all confidence that anyone who violates the sovereignty of Germany will face a storm of steel. The socialist minister R. Has said that youth must accept the fact that Marxists rule over them. The youth, whose best part holds AKS membership, cannot possibly do so, even though much of our bourgeoisie appears to have done so with remarkable ease. We refuse to accept this, especially since the Marxists, along with their bourgeois allies refuse to build an army that would guarantee our independence. It is nationalists who must create a military power to be reckoned with, here in the extreme North.

We now argue if income taxes should be raised by 15 or 25% to cover the expenses required for basic upgrades. Certain bourgeois elements fight against any additional taxes with all their might. It seems possible that it is the educated class that will suffer the most due to the increased taxes, although they now already pay more taxes than all the other social classes combined, including farmers, industrial workers, and traders. But even if the difficulty cannot be evenly distributed, it must be taken on and suffered without complaint. If all we are left with is a beggar's cup, let that be our lot, as long as our army is strong. We must rally all our strength as they are doing in Russia. What is the purpose of funding culture, when we have nothing to defend our culture with? All the work, all the sacrifice we all have made for this country can come to nothing in an instant if our defenses are too weak to protect all our achievements. A people who squabble over pennies while their national defense languishes has no permanent place in the hall of nations.

Almost every AKS carries an officer's permit. The most important task of this militant association is the militarization of our youth. No sacrifice is too great for this purpose. There is no other way to prepare for the moment when the bombers of the Eastern superpower block out the sun.

The Weakness of Finland's National Defenses

Parliamentary Remarks, April 29, 1938

The ministry of finance has presented a program of improvements for our national defense. However, the needs of our navy have been completely ignored. Therefore, I would like to discuss this matter briefly.

The navy is an extremely important branch of service, so it is profoundly odd that the committee does not suggest any funds for reinforcing it. They bypass the entire issue by stating that the plan for developing the navy is still unfinished at the time of the committee meeting, so the committee recommends that the government urgently resolve the issue. This despite the fact that the committee has at its disposal the documents dating May 1, 1924, which form the basis of the very issue the government has ordered the committee to resolve. This minimum program for improving the navy, decided upon by the government, has only been partially carried out so far, despite all the experts approving of it. Most lamentably of all, the destroyers included in the program have not been built. Therefore, we still have no destroyers of our own, now that the destroyers captured from the Russians have been decommissioned.

The experts say that we need a minimum of two destroyers per coastal battleship in order for them to be able to carry out their missions effectively. The committee should at the very least have been aware of this and recommended we allocate funds to rectify this serious shortcoming in our naval defense, even if they otherwise wish to leave this matter for the government.

It is true that a navy is an expensive form of defense. It is nevertheless absolutely necessary, due to our long coastlines and naval trade routes. It has been remarked that if there are no funds made available for this purpose, all the money spent on other forms of defense will be wasted as well. I have been told that the destroyers our navy presently needs can be built at a cost of approximately 75 million marks each.

When this matter was last discussed in parliament, MP F.[84] suggested, that one of our most capable naval officers be named the commander of our navy and promoted to the rank of admiral. He was laughed at, but the fact remains that our navy lacks a capable, authoritative commander. Our entire navy is classified in the organization of our defense forces as a regiment, meaning its head officer would correspond to a lieutenant colonel. This is an excellent example of the negligence from which this extremely important branch of our defense currently suffers.

We never would have gotten underway in building a navy for independent Finland at all, if not for the sinking of old torpedo S2, which took 53 young sailors with her to the deep. So what else do we need to see happen for the government to realize the importance of this issue? For them to understand that our neighboring nation has the world's largest fleet of submarines? It is of the utmost importance that the government follow the suggestion of the defense funding committee and begins to develop our navy as soon as possible.

Another important issue that has also been previously discussed here is that of fortifying the Åland Islands. This should also have been covered in the basic program. It has been said that our greatest weakness is a demilitarized Åland. Åland is the key to our sea routes. Who holds Åland, controls them. Åland is a magnet that will immediately attract all major powers, should war break out. We can only imagine what Åland under the control of some hostile power would mean if they were to use it as a naval and airbase. We should also take into consideration that with modern military methods, Åland can be overtaken in a matter of

---

[84] It is unclear who the "Member of Parliament F." mentioned here is. There were several MP's at the time whose surname begins with F.

hours, since the enemy has at its disposal airborne saboteurs. We must take immediate action to remove ourselves from the demilitarization pact of Åland. There are unofficial reports that this is already underway, but our absolute demand must be that Åland, as Finnish territory, is fortified by Finland alone. Otherwise, it is better to leave it as it currently is. We must not give in to any demands that, as the Swedish press puts it, this be done in a manner "acceptable to Sweden and Scandinavia." Let us remember that it was our western neighbor that demolished the previous fortifications in Åland. It has been painful to see to what extent the discussion here has been based on purely monetary considerations when the matter at hand is our national defense.

Our parliamentary group has already announced that we shall accept the proposal for these basic military expenses. It is true that the additional tax this requires will be a heavy burden for the educated middle class, but this is caused by our system of taxation itself, not the matter at hand here. At a geopolitically critical time, when nations are gathering all their forces and preparing for the gigantic battle to come, we must do so too, and by doing so we may not always be able to distribute the extra burden as equally as ideally we should. In my opinion, the government's proposal has at least attempted to minimize the hardship caused to the poor, who in turn had to suffer excessively in the recent years of crisis.

It is therefore tragic to see this matter being used as an excuse for worthless agitation, and on the other hand, for pointlessly mocking those who have to loosen their purse strings. Our taxation is not excessive. If our information is correct, the Soviet Union spends in excess of 3,000 marks per capita in armaments annually, when here it is only 300 marks. We consider the financial ministry's proposal of 2,710 million marks unsatisfactory and believe that the defense committee's proposals should have been accepted as they are. But I suppose that we should be content with what we have, especially since even the Social Democrats support the proposal, even if it's due to "fear of fascism," as they insist on reminding us. Therefore, fascism has indirectly done our country a great favor by scaring the Social Democrats away from their customary nihilism when it comes to national defense. We hope that once these funds have been used as efficiently as possible and the sorry state of our navy and fortifications amended, our minister of defense's claim will actually be true: that any enemy invasion to our country will be no flag parade.

A Promise for the Future

Mustapaidat Kuortaneummer Camp, June 28, 1938

On my way to this event, I paused for a moment to watch some gas protection exercises that were going on the athletics field. My attention was especially drawn to a phosphorus bomb crackling in the sand. The more they tried to put it out, the brighter it burned. Water was poured on it, it was covered with sand, but as soon as it was touched by the wind, it burst back into a new flame, even under a layer of sand.

While watching this, the parallels to nationalist awakening in the hearts of the Blackshirt youth became obvious. It also burns all the brighter for all the attempts to extinguish it. Its fire has been kept going through all the attempts of the ruling class to put it out. As the phosphorus bomb could not be extinguished with sand or water, as long as is in contact with air, equally the wind of nationalist awakening blows through their hearts, keeping up this inextinguishable flame. An attempt was made to prevent these lads from congregating here in this municipality. And what was the result? Again our footsteps have been heard, as the song of the Mustapaidat (Blackshirts) rings out for all to hear.

A torrential rain has washed over us, and some were foolish enough to think that this would be enough to dilute the spirit of our camp. Everyone here can easily testify that this has not been the case. Even in wind and rain, soaked to the bone, our youth have marched with excitement and determination in their eyes. And they will march again here to Kuortane[85] in the coming years, even if they have to make camp at the swamp. Would the system

---

[85] Kuortane is a municipality in the Ostrobothnia region in southwestern Finland.

be successful in dividing the nationalist youth, even if they ban one of their official organizations, the Mustapaidat? They have held their camps more often than ever before. Their conscience will never permit them to think that any of the excuses used to deal with the death of that organization are truly criminal. If they must be forced to admit that their passion for Greater Finland is criminal, they simultaneously accuse of criminality those lads who through three years of war gave their lives in Karelia. They will never submit to this. To them, their comrades who fell in Karelia are their greatest heroes and examples, and they vow to walk in their footsteps until Karelia and Ingria are free.

Furthermore, it was said that the Blackshirt organization has behaved in an improper way for supporting an "attempted coup" in Estonia. But if this is a reason to ban and forbid an organization, then all of the youth of this country must be banned and criminalized. For all of Finland's youth sympathizes with this strike against the vilest violence, betrayal, and inequity imaginable. May the Lord help Finland's youth, if they lose a sense of justice and righteous fury toward evil and violence! You, inhabitants of Kuortane, have gathered here in this hut, as if in some cabin hidden in the woods. There are more of us here than this dwelling can comfortably admit. But why is it, exactly, that you have all come here? So you could light a fire in your heart that is brighter than phosphorus, or anything else for that matter. Moreover, you keep that flame going in us old freedom and tribal fighters, men whose time some think already has passed. They keep the flame going even in the present times of depression and materialism, and therefore are the only true promise of a brighter future. In reality, this youth are the most precious gift to the people of Finland, who should really thank the Lord for them on their knees, rather than despise them. The present refuses to acknowledge this, but history will one day vindicate them.

The Youth Who Still Believe in Life

Mustapaidat Meeting in Urjala, September 4, 1938

The youth gathered here have been called wild, undisciplined, and we, the leaders of such youth, demagogues and mountebanks. This is a label we carry proudly because in this country, youth who have undergone a nationalist awakening have always been accused of demagoguery. At the very least, these youngsters compare very favorably with youth who waste the most precious years of a person's life, with no ideals, with no goals. In the recent past, our youth lived almost entirely without higher ideals of any kind. It was ready to drown in the waves of cosmopolitan European culture washing over us. It was gnawed from within by despair. They believed in nothing but the ever-changing present, yet they wished to grab and hold onto anything they could. What good do such youth do to anyone?

On the other hand, the youth gathered here, who call themselves the Blackshirts, have a completely different and much nobler outlook. They believe in life again; they have renewed ideals and a guiding star to follow. This guiding star is called Fatherland. For this ideal, they have shown themselves willing to sacrifice their youth, even their life. I only hope that in addition, the southern wind of a spiritual awakening may also soon blow through their ranks. And there already are some signs that this is indeed happening. Then the liberation of Karelia and Ingria would also not be far, the "Anschluss" of the Finnic tribe. It is toward this moment that the Blackshirt youth continue to struggle. It is because of this that they always gather under the flags of Finland, Estonia, and Karelia. Earlier today, I was deeply moved as I watched how they raised their arms in salute, as our tribal banners were raised. I remember how the ranks of lads grew thinner as we fought in Karelia and how the flags were lowered for good in Pepola, Porajärvi, and Kirjasalo. Now the ranks under these banners have been reinforced, a new youth steps in to fill the ranks of fallen comrades, and their song is heard, like from their lips as from the Spanish Falangists: "I march with my brothers, those who watch us from the stars, who know our pain. Should I fall, my place too shall be there."

The Men of the Freedom War

Veterans' Pre-Christmas Gathering,
Kiuruvesi, December 18, 1938

Brothers in arms! We war veterans should be grateful for the ladies' auxiliary troops for organizing events such as this pre-Christmas gathering. It is moments like this that allow us, who are united by shared memories, to gather. Meetings like these can have a larger significance than we may think. We are always reminded of what we have in common, and our differences always pale in comparison. We belong to different social classes, we represent different worldviews and political factions, but we have something that transcends every division — brotherhood in arms. Only those who walked the fields of death in 1918 can fully understand everything the men of the front lines share. We are united by shared suffering twenty years ago, by shared joy and grief, by victories and defeats. We all had to throw ourselves into the same snowbanks, rich and poor, all in the same gray uniforms. There we found ourselves compelled to follow the Lord's command: "If anyone has material possessions and sees a brother or sister in need but has no pity on them, how can the love of God be in that person?"

We were ready to clothe a shivering comrade with an item of clothing that we ourselves needed. Should we still find some frozen bread crust in the bottom of our pack, we chewed on it together, awake in the night, under the unforgiving stars. "Greater love has no one than this: to lay down one's life for one's friends." This was the sermon given by our field pastor, in a battle that began not long after some youths had to risk their own lives in order to save their wounded comrades from the enemy fire.

Their own lives meant nothing when it came to rescuing their comrades from bleeding to death. Many gave their own lives for their companions, twenty years ago. This gathering includes men from every front of the freedom war: Satakunta, Tavastia, the siege of Tampere, from Savonia and from Karelia, even some who fought in White Sea Karelia, Olonets and Estonia. But the experiences are the same, regardless of where they took place.

A great number of the men who then fought, now live in great material need and poverty. In this parish alone, an overwhelming majority of front-line fighters belong to the poor class. In the past 20 years, these men have continued to serve their country by starting large families and thus advancing the life of our nation. Many front veterans have sacrificed their best years for their families, but still, poverty and need haunt their homes, and the meager meals of their children are seasoned with tears. In the heart of the neighboring parish, there is a veteran family of 8 children, some of them blind, who have no better home than a small peat hut. In a remote village of Iisalmi, a veteran has to house his large family in a sauna. This family was visited by a priest, who took it upon himself to ask the veteran why he would not ask for assistance. The father of the family replied, "When I was in Helsinki last spring, for the 20th anniversary of the freedom war, our former commander Mannerheim said: you veterans must not walk with your heads bowed, but hold them high. I would rather starve than beg because I must obey my commander and hold my head up high, and beggars must walk with bowed heads."

The veterans did not fight for financial gain or to attain a privileged position in society. They simply did their duty, without asking for money or glory. Nevertheless, our society owes a debt of honor to our veterans. It must take care that our veterans are not forced to walk with bowed heads. A Nation that does not honor the most glorious parts of its history will be erased from the pages of history. Recently more attention has been paid to these matters, but much still remains to be done. We salute the organizations that have undertaken this voluntary work of assisting the veterans. The veterans themselves must make sure that they do not become reliant on this assistance, but continue to do everything in their power to provide for themselves and their families. Any one of them who fails to do so has allowed the fire that burned in their hearts to go out. The ranks of the veterans grow thinner year by year. More and more often we must bare our heads before the casket of a comrade. The day when only a handful remain is not far now. The group that has already joined our comrades who fell in the freedom war grows, and similarly those of us who remain grow fewer. Nevertheless, we look hopefully to the future. There is a new youth who follow us and replace the missing many times over. With burning hearts, the youth have recited poetry and sang songs in order to lift the all too often sunken spirits of the veterans. And they are ready to step onto the fields of death when that time yet again comes when the Fatherland's fate is once again at stake. Let us hope that the day is far in the future. But if it is instead close, this old veteran will again stand under the same banners with the youth, in order to once again give it all for the Fatherland.

Through Strife

Mustapaidat Rally, Helsinki, April 26, 1939

The geopolitical situation has become extremely strained as of late. At one moment there was a point of pressure that was alarmingly sliding toward the Gulf of Finland. The Soviet Union offered to become a "protector" for Estonia, with Estonia responding to this kind offer by beginning construction of concrete and steel fortifications on its islands. Finland was also subject to pressure from the Soviets, and our response to this was… begin drafting *a law* for defending the republic. Since after all, we are not allowed to fortify our vulnerable islands, based on the Tarto agreement, an agreement which some present government ministers helped to draft. The Åland Islands cannot be fortified for reasons we all know well, and even during this time of crisis, a delegation from Åland departed with the intention of selling curly birch to the chief secretary of the League of Nations. If we were to examine the politics of weakness which Finland has fallen into, usually at times of turmoil, it would be difficult to not feel the most profound depression. In fact, the entire people of Finland carry a mark of collective national weakness. It has never achieved greatness except in the deepest suffering.

It is now 20 years since the freedom struggle of Olonets began. The goddess of history held out the keys of greatness for our people. But we allowed the troops of youthful volunteers to be destroyed by the Russians' grenade launchers. And we speak of the same youth, who reminded the correspondent of a magazine from Copenhagen of the Garibaldinos in the battle for the freedom of Italy. Living this national atrophy we have enviously watched the robust flame of nationalism in Hungary, our brother nation. They have not let up for a moment in their struggle, and as a consequence, the shackles of Trianon are now breaking from their shoulders. One can see that this is a fighting people, with a glorious history that we do not have. They have forged into their souls the national will and faith, which Petöf expressed in verse. The phrase "Nem, nem, soha!" is tattooed in the soul of every Hungarian. It has simply been a matter of waiting for the right moment to place everything on the scales of history for the greatness of Hungary, and therefore in the great historical play, the call of "Rise, Magyar, your nation is calling!" has been heard from the eternal slopes of the Carpathians. At the same time, a youth organization is banned in Finland, with the justification of "A positive attitude toward the question of Greater Finland, and the quasi-military discipline present within it."

In Lapua, at the grave of the heroic fallen, a young priest addressed his congregation thus: "The best youth organization of Finland has just been banned." Someone might be tempted to remark that he is one of these fanatic, fascist priests. Even if he is, he has the right to speak, as two of his comrades rest in the grave at which he speaks. Wild rumors spread in Helsinki when one and another great power is planning to invade. Only at such a moment, when the only question is which great power will be the first to send their battleships into the Gulf of Finland, does the government make their decisive move: *a proposal for a law to protect the republic*. The purpose of this law has been described in the most patriotic terms by the cabinet ministers and the parties to which these ministers belong. It has been a special point of lamentation, that the government, which does not especially love limiting personal freedoms or passing dictatorial laws, finds itself forced to do so now.

Everyone of course understands that the purpose is a dictatorial one: the destruction of the IKL. The measures taken in November are supposedly justified by the fact that some schoolboys blew up a zinc bucket outside the People's House of

Kuopio. This latest affront to the freedoms of speech, congregation, and opinion of certain citizens is based on foreign policy. The magazine *Soihtu*[86] does not shy away from telling the truth in this matter. An article they published describes the whole preposterous truth. In place of the courts, which as of yet have not been "aired out," the golden scales of justice will instead be worked by the Parliament. They write:

> *It is also notable that this law will allow the development of societal conditions toward greater democracy, because it will transfer power in many decisive matters from the courts, which are controlled by the right-wing, to the parliament.*

Here we see the Parliament wielding its newfound powers. Over there on the left, which this so-called court leans toward, I see judges whose theoretical skills are rudimentary at best, but who are not lacking in practical experience.

Some might call this biting sarcasm. It may be, but if only it were so biting that it would bite through to the heart of this people's conscience. And still, here we are at the stage many of us have longed for. For every movement for national liberation has had to break through to victory through incarcerations, bans, and difficulties. A man of honor must never back down in the face of violence. Violence has at times in the past been blessed with the signet of the law, but that does not mean it is no longer violence. The author of our national awakening, J. V. Snellman spoke words I would have written in indelible ink on our souls: "If the public citizen is bowed by orders which are not law, but rather clearly in contradiction of the law, he denies his own understanding of justice."

It may also happen that injustice steals the signet of law and the public citizen, as an honorable man, must take this into account as well. We must remember that above all human justice

---

[86] *Torch* was a leftist student magazine. It was published between 1931–1991.

or injustice there is an eternal, unwavering truth that delivers judgments that cannot be influenced by bribes. Believing in this, fighting for it, we can pass through the harshest difficulties. It is possible that the IKL will not be crowned with the victor's laurels. But it is not for any particular organization that we fight for, but for an immeasurably higher ideal: for the Fatherland. Each one of us should be able to give even a drop of that which is eternal in us for God and country, for else a human life is spent in vain, and time is short. When Luther departed for Worms, his friends warmed him that he may lose his life and even the cause of the evangelism will be lost. To this Luther replied: "It is unimportant what happens to one Dr. Martin, and I suppose it is possible that I may not be able to save the cause of evangelism, but the point is that the truth be heard."

It is equally inconsequential what happens to each of us personally or what happens to the IKL, but rather that the truth be spoken in our time as well.